VINCENZO VENEZIA

fearful avoidant attachment

Managing Hot/Cold Behaviours, Improving Emotional Intimacy Issues, and Building Deep Connections with Your Partner

ISBN: 979-12-81498-15-0

TABLE OF CONTENTS

INTRODUCTION

We desire to love and be loved by others because it is the most beautiful feeling in the world. In the past, people went through a very long process of courtship before getting married, which was a good thing because it gave ample time for the guy and the girl to get to know each other better and determine if they are a good match in terms of personality and values. However, today's world is different from what we had a few decades ago. Nowadays, it is more common to fall in love with someone you just met instead of someone you've known for years. Social media has made it simpler than ever to connect with someone who lives far away, or even your next-door neighbor. This technological advancement has made it easier for people to meet and develop relationships.

However, not everyone is good at developing relationships. Some find it hard to maintain a relationship because they have never learned how to love and be loved by someone else. In their case, they are more comfortable by themselves. They would rather be alone than risk giving their heart away just to get hurt when the relationship ends up being unsuccessful. They often suffer from fear of abandonment, which makes them avoid getting into a relationship at all costs. They are too afraid of being abandoned to love someone else. They tend to avoid relationships because they fear getting attached and losing their independence. Yes, they want to love, but they don't want it badly enough that they will give up their independence and freedom for it.

The attachment they had when they were young may have left a very bad mark on their minds that can only be soothed having complete independence. Because of this, they often treat everyone coldly because they don't want to be emotionally attached to anyone. When they fall in love with someone else, some of them will even go as far as wanting to harm themselves out of fear of losing control and losing their freedom.

Fearful avoidant attachment is a real problem for many people. One of the most prevalent emotional disorders that causes someone to experience a great deal of emotional pain, this crippling disorder needs to be addressed as soon as possible.

The good news is that it is possible to change this dysfunctional pattern of behavior. The way out of this emotional disorder is by replacing the old fear-based behavior with a more rational one that recognizes the need for healthy relationships but does not fully depend on them for survival. This book is written to help you to overcome your fear of abandonment and develop a healthy relationship that is not dependent on emotional attachments.

This book will teach you how to let go of the fear of being abandoned and learn to have a healthy relationship that allows you to love and be loved by someone else. It will help you become a better partner. You will also learn how to give love and get love back when you need it. This book will also teach you to stop blaming others for their lack of emotional ability, their emotional problems, and their lack of willingness to change.

Most importantly, this book will teach you that you are not the only one who suffers from a fearful avoidant attachment. Millions of people worldwide suffer from this same disorder, and it doesn't have to be that way. This book is your chance to feel the love you want in all your relationships. If you're ready to learn how to love, this book is for you.

Knowledge is power. You can deal with something better once you understand it. You will be happier once you understand what you are missing in your life. Your fear of being abandoned will no longer hold power over you. After reading this book, nothing will be the same again.

PART 1

AN INTRODUCTION TO FEARFUL AVOIDANT ATTACHMENT

CHAPTER 1

WHAT IS ATTACHMENT THEORY?

Attachments are emotional bonds between people created by normal interactions that result in either positive or negative feelings for one another. The term 'attachment' is also used to describe how children try to attach themselves to something (or someone) to feel better, safer, or more comfortable.

Humans are social creatures that rely on their relationships with others to survive and thrive. We are born with a built-in need to attach or bond with those around us, and those bonds (or lack thereof) can greatly impact our ability to feel secure in the world around us. This desire to bond with others is not just normal but also instinctive. The need to attach or bond with those closest to us is part of what makes us human.

John Bowlby's Attachment Theory

Psychoanalyst John Bowlby (1907–1990) developed the now-famous theory that explains how these connections between someone and those around them come to be. Because he is acknowledged as having introduced and popularized the idea of attachment theory in the West, he is frequently referred to as "the father of attachment theory."

Ethological theory in general, but particularly Konrad Lorenz's 1935 study of imprinting, had a significant impact on Bowlby. In young ducklings, Lorenz demonstrated that attachment was innate and therefore had a survival value. Lorenz used the terms 'imprinting' and 'programmed behavior' to describe this effect, which he saw as part of natural selection. Bowlby was convinced that the same principle applied to human babies and sought to demonstrate that emotional bonds were innate and evolved through natural selection since they ensure the survival of the young.

More importantly, Bowlby used the term 'attachment' (that he borrowed from field biology) to describe these emotional bonds, thus introducing a new concept in psychology.

Attachment theory has three central aspects:

1. Attachment is Biologically Based and Wired into Our Genes

According to Bowlby, the need to form attachments to others is a product of evolution, wired into our genes. In other words, it is a characteristic of being human that ensures our survival and provides us with a feeling of security and comfort in any situation. Bowlby believed that this instinctive drive is present from birth and is a product of evolution since it greatly increases our chances of survival.

Bowlby believed that the human brain is wired from birth to function in a particular way, and that we are naturally drawn to seek safety and comfort in those close to us. Our brains instinctively tell us to look for things in our environment (or those around us) that are likely to provide safety and comfort, so we seek out those who offer this comfort most effectively. These people become the center of our universe, the objects of our instinctive drive to seek security and comfort, and as a result, the bonds we form with them are very powerful.

Bowlby believed there is a biological basis for these relationships since they are not entirely learned from others but also discovered through experience. This means that humans are born with the same instinctive drive to seek comfort and security from those around us as other animals.

2. Infants Have an Early Need to Form Attachments or Bonds with Their Caregivers.

Attachment is a very powerful instinct that starts early in life.

The attachment bond can be formed via two methods:

1. The caregiver's proximity ensures the young child's comfort since proximity (being close) is essential for comfort.

2. The caregiver's ability to support the child's basic needs (food, warmth, etc.) ensures the child's safety.

Consequently, infants' attachment to their caregivers starts as soon as they are born and is an instinctive or innate drive that is necessary for their survival.

3. Our Attachment Needs Are Not Only Aimed at Our Caregivers but Also Those Around Us.

After discovering the idea of attachment, Bowlby noticed that infants form attachments to several people. These can include their parents, siblings, extended family members (grandparents, aunts, and uncles), and close friends. Anyone we have regular contact with can become an attachment figure. How we form attachments is based on regular contact with someone rather than on the person's ability to support our basic needs.

These three aspects of attachment are the key concepts in attachment theory and explain how and why humans develop deep connections or bonds with those around us. This is a very important part of human nature and one we are designed to do naturally, but this also means we can potentially form unhealthy relationships with others.

Secure Attachment in Childhood

The healthiest form of attachment is secure attachment. It describes an attachment in which a child is comforted by the presence of their caregiver and, as a result, is confident that they will continue to be cared for by the same individual in the future.

How Does Secure Attachment Develop?

There are two conditions leading to the development of secure attachment:

1. The mother must be sensitive to her infant's signals.

The first condition for developing secure attachment is that the mother/caregiver must be sensitive to the infant's signals. This means they must react properly if their child cries or makes any distress signal. The mother or caregiver gives assurance and comfort that she will always be there for the child in times of need by appropriately responding to their needs. It is a good base from which the child can explore their environment without feeling abandoned or frightened.

This is vital in developing and maintaining secure attachment since if the mother/caregiver fails to sense her child's needs or fears, they will learn that they are not safe and their needs may not be met. In such circumstances, infants become afraid and look for a new attachment figure or base, which could be a substitute for their mother/caregiver, but is likely to be an inanimate object (e.g., a blanket) or part of their mother/caregiver such as a smell.

2. The infant must feel safe with their caregiver.

The second condition for developing secure attachment is that the child feels secure with their mother/caregiver. It is not enough that the mother/caregiver is sensitive to their child's signals; they must also provide physical comfort and reassurance and allow their child to explore in an environment of safety. In order for the baby to learn how to take care of themselves emotionally and physically, the mother or caregiver uses a style of caregiving known as responsive caregiving, which entails letting the baby explore their environment freely and at their own pace. When this occurs, infants develop confidence that they will always be cared for by the same person in the future, which is essential for a secure base.

These two components of secure attachment are vital in helping infants develop healthy relationships with others and themselves. When these requisite conditions are met, children grow up to form secure attachments with others, and this allows them to feel confident enough to explore the world around them and potentially work collaboratively with others.

The Importance of Secure Attachment in Childhood

The following are the reasons why having a secure attachment in childhood is important to adult relationships.

Securely attached children can:

1. Develop Self-Regulation

Securely attached children have the ability to develop the skills necessary for maintaining a happy, healthy lifestyle and coping appropriately with stressful situations. This includes knowing how to deal with problems and stressors in their daily lives, such as being upset by someone's behavior or failing an exam. Securely attached children know they will be supported if they are faced with these struggles and maintain a calm, productive state even in difficult times. They can stay calm and focused on their goals without becoming frustrated or frightened, keeping them on track for the long-term outcome of accomplishing the task or achieving the desired result. Securely attached children face life with an optimistic outlook and look at their surroundings as a good place, as opposed to fearing what may come around the corner. This gives them the self-confidence needed to cope with challenges and expectations when it comes to achieving or reaching goals in general.

To demonstrate…

When a child goes through a traumatic ordeal, they are likely to feel scared and distressed. However, because they have a strong, secure attachment with their parent/caregiver, they can maintain calm and confidence and handle the situation appropriately. Knowing their feelings and boundaries allows them to let out all their emotions appropriately while still controlling themselves, keeping them on track for future success and achievement. This means they can experience a positive outlook in life and deal with any future struggles or negative events, and will grow up to be more confident, optimistic, competent, and willing to work collaboratively with others.

2. Develop Positive Relationships

Securely attached children can develop positive relationships with their peers and siblings as they are confident enough to build strong relationships with others that will last a lifetime. This does not mean that children must actively seek out friends, as this is not always the case for many children in complex environments such as our modern world, where someone may have different agendas due to the lack of opportunity or resources at home or because of discrimination by others. Nonetheless, children who have a strong relationship with their parents can accept those from other families and will be happier if they are surrounded by friends who are supportive of their goals and values. This means that children will generally be less likely to feel isolated and more comfortable coming out of their shells, as well as more likely to cooperate with others.

To demonstrate...

When a child is rejected by peers or has problems with their peers, they may feel vulnerable, lonely, and insecure. However, because they have a secure attachment with their parent/caregiver, the child will be more able to cope in these situations and less likely to end up feeling distressed, withdrawn, or upset. They will trust that the parent will help them figure out how to manage the issue and support them through their problems without undermining their confidence. This creates an environment where children are more inclined to reach out for help if needed rather than suffering in silence on their own and feeling more confident to deal with any challenges.

3. Able to Handle Conflict

Securely attached children can manage conflict resolution as they are able to remain calm and confident during challenging situations, even when they disagree with their parents. They also feel confident that they will be supported by the same caregiver in the future and know that they will not be abandoned. Children with secure attachment grow up to be more confident, curious, and willing to explore the world around them. They are also more able to learn from the adversities that arise in their lives and are better able to tolerate challenges and stressful events.

To demonstrate...

A child may have a disagreement with their parents and still feel unsure of the consequences or how to act appropriately. However, because they have a secure attachment with their parent/caregiver, the child will be able to remain calm and relaxed throughout the situation and confront any conflict with a cooperative attitude. This will allow them to remain calm and confident and reach an appropriate conclusion and learn from their mistakes instead of feeling angry or frustrated.

4. Develop a Sense of Self and Identity

Children develop into adults by developing a sense of self, which includes their feelings and values. Securely attached children have learned they can depend on others to be there for them when needed and that they can connect with others. They become more secure in their sense of self and develop a strong identity, and feel confident enough to work with others while maintaining a standard of values that they feel comfortable with.

To demonstrate...

Children who have a secure attachment relationship with their caregiver are more likely to feel free to express themselves without worrying about what other people think of them, leading them to develop a stronger sense of self.

5. Enjoy Age-Appropriate Behaviors and Relationships

Another benefit of secure attachment is that the child will develop age-appropriate behaviors and relationships without feeling worried, tense, or confused. Children who have a strong sense of self will not only be able to enjoy the company of friends and family better but will also allow themselves to relax around others who can be trusted enough not to hurt them in any way. They gain more confidence in their ability to deal with the pressures of being a teenager and to grow up successfully.

To demonstrate…

Securely attached children are more likely to enjoy age-appropriate activities and relationships with others in their society. This entails having fun while playing games or working on assignments, finishing household chores, and taking part in activities like sports or music lessons without feeling overly anxious or insecure. They will be able to express themselves confidently and openly.

6. Understand the Importance of Others and Self-Care

Securely attached children can understand that they are important to others. Children develop confidence in their ability to make friends, form peer groups, and interact with others, which helps them when they grow older. Furthermore, they will be more likely to take care of their physical needs such as sleeping, eating, or using the toilet when necessary.

To demonstrate...

Children with a secure attachment understand that others are important and will not ignore them in favor of accomplishments. They may notice when their friends need help with an assignment and will choose to do things together. This can lead children to enjoy their relationships with parents, peers, and friends, and to take care of themselves when necessary, ultimately forming healthy relationships that can last many years.

7. Develop Social Competence

Social competence is a major part of a healthy childhood and is a required skill in adulthood. Securely attached children can develop social competence as they can appropriately connect with others, express themselves effectively, and understand their feelings. Because of these skills, securely attached children can easily foster friendships and relationships throughout their childhood and beyond and will be more likely to make friends easily throughout adulthood.

To demonstrate...

Children with a strong sense of self can make friends easily, and develop friendships that last throughout their lives. They also understand their emotions well enough to cope with negative situations. They are also confident enough in their relationships with others that they do not feel anxiety or fear when close relationships do not last and cannot bear the pain of losing someone they care about.

Young adults who have developed social skills based on a secure attachment become more confident in their abilities as adults. Their confidence in themselves can help them initiate new relationships or be more comfortable mingling with other individuals without feeling overly insecure or shy. This can help them achieve their career and personal goals better, which will help them throughout the rest of their lives.

8. Are Mentally Healthier

Children who develop secure attachment become more healthy in adulthood than those who have insecure attachment. Securely attached children can better understand their relationships with others, express themselves confidently, and are more at ease around others throughout their lives. This can help them to form healthy relationships later on and achieve their personal and career goals. This will help them feel good about themselves as an adult and avoid depression or anxiety.

To demonstrate...

Children who have a secure attachment and understand how to bond with others will feel good about themselves and be more at ease even when their relationships do not last. They can better cope with negative situations as they are confident that they can depend on others. This makes it easier for them to learn from their mistakes and make good decisions as they age.

Children who develop a secure attachment can be mentally healthier as adults; however, this does not mean that all children with a secure attachment will be mentally healthy in adulthood. Many factors contribute to mental health in adulthood, and it is possible to have a secure attachment and still have problems growing up or even in adulthood, depending on other factors that affect mental health.

9. Lead a Healthier Life

The ability to form secure attachments can significantly impact an individual's health in adulthood by helping them cope with negative situations in their lives by taking care of themselves and being confident enough in their abilities to make good choices. Adults are less likely to abuse alcohol or drugs; they can express themselves more confidently and know that if they are hurt or do something wrong, there is someone who will support them through any negative consequences they may experience.

To demonstrate...

Someone with a secure attachment can take better care of themselves and cope with negative situations throughout their lives better than those who do not have a secure attachment. Children who develop a secure attachment learn that others care about them, making them feel good about themselves. This can help them avoid drug use, drinking, and smoking, as well as other negative health habits such as overeating or not eating enough to stay healthy.

10. Develop a Mix of Self-Esteem and Realism

Children who form a strong bond with their parents can form realistic self-perceptions, which will help them feel good about themselves as adults. They will be realistic about what they can accomplish, and able to deal with their emotions with confidence. This can help them to have a more positive outlook on life, and they will find it easier to deal with the challenges of trying to make something of themselves as an adult.

To demonstrate...

Children who develop a secure attachment can express themselves confidently, understand the importance of taking care of themselves, and know that they must meet their own expectations if they want things to work out for them. Academic performance, the amount of effort they put into their studies, and whether or not they have reasonable expectations for the future can all be greatly impacted by self-care and the use of strategies like self-talk and positive thinking.

Someone with a secure attachment can be realistic and have a positive outlook on life while still being confident in their abilities. They may feel good about themselves and expect the best, but they do not expect more than what they can accomplish through hard work, self-discipline, and their own special gifts. They can also recognize their weaknesses and shortcomings while still being confident enough to work hard every day to overcome these problems. This can help them to avoid feeling bad about themselves because of mistakes or bad situations that result from things outside of their control.

11. Develop a Better Understanding of Love

Children who develop a secure attachment can better understand the importance of love and how it affects their feelings, security, and well-being as adults. When children can form a secure relationship with their primary attachment figures in childhood, they learn that they should depend on others during difficult times, and they can be comforted when they are hurt or upset. This can help them be more confident in how they express themselves and communicate with others.

To demonstrate...

Children who form secure attachments learn how to rely on others. This can help them throughout their lives, especially when they experience negative situations. Someone who has a secure attachment will have an easier time expressing themselves because of their understanding of the importance of love and support from others. This can help them to be more confident when communicating with others, and help them get along better with their families, and develop closer relationships with those around them.

Having a secure attachment as a child can make it easier for an individual to work through negative situations and develop healthier, more successful relationships. While not all children who grow up with secure attachments become successful adults, most do. The connections made between children and their primary attachment figures form the basis for how they will lead their lives as adults and can lead to healthier, happier lives.

CHAPTER 2

WHAT IS FEARFUL AVOIDANT ATTACHMENT?

Fearful avoidant attachment (also known as 'anxious-avoidant attachment') is a term for someone who craves love and connection but is also preoccupied with rejection. This is a form of attachment disorder that shows up in someone's early childhood. Fearful avoidance is usually quite severe and can be associated with other fears, phobias, and anxieties that are difficult to resolve and are thus carried through to adulthood.

Characteristics of Someone with Fearful Avoidant Attachment

The following is a list of the qualities that someone with fearful avoidant attachment displays and how they might behave in different situations:

1. Shallow Emotions

Fearful avoidants may have very shallow feelings. They may display anger or frustration, but they can quickly diffuse them again. They will often feel very insecure and may not have a stable sense of identity. They will also have their fears, inhibitions, and tensions, which may be masked by their constant need to look happy and confident. Because they do not feel that they can express their emotions in a way that makes them feel safe, the avoidance aspect of fearful avoidant attachment is the typical way of dealing with life's problems.

They may seem cool and calm, but in reality, they have no idea how to handle the real issues that they face. They frequently use extreme, black-and-white thinking. Everyday circumstances can be extremely murky and complex, including situations wherein their partner is concerned about their feelings and needs. Even if they are told that they are loved, they will still not feel capable of telling their partner how much they care or the true extent of their feelings.

2. Lack of Confidence

Fearful avoidants can display a lack of confidence, which can be seen in their hobbies and interests. They may have a lack of enthusiasm for things they used to look forward to. This is because they don't feel as though they deserve the same rewards that others get; they don't feel as though they are a worthy person. This lack of confidence in their abilities is also reflected in their relationships.

These individuals may have as much knowledge about a topic as anyone else, but they may seem uninterested and unwilling to share that knowledge. They are often more concerned with being polite and helpful than being direct about what they think or know. They may not believe that their opinions or expertise is valuable. It is very difficult for them to let others help them because it seems like such an admission of failure and lack of faith in oneself. They will also feel a bit of guilt if something good happens to them, as they do not think that they necessarily deserve it.

3. Isolated and Lonely

One of the biggest challenges for fearful avoidants is that they are typically very lonely. The isolation and loneliness can be emotionally devastating and can create enormous anxiety. This is because they do not feel that they have anyone who loves them or cares about them. Despite having lots of acquaintances, they have few friends and nobody to whom they can confide their most private feelings. There is a strong urge for these individuals to find someone who can provide them with the love, acceptance, and support that will finally make them feel worthy of love and capable of loving others in return. The fact that many fearful avoidant individuals do not have well-developed social skills can also contribute to feeling isolated.

4. Excessive Self-Consciousness

This personality type is usually quiet, reserved, and thoughtful. They prefer to observe and analyze situations instead of becoming directly involved in situations. They are very aware of their environment. They are very self-conscious about their appearance in public or with others. This can often make them appear shy or aloof. It can also make it difficult for these individuals to be assertive if they feel they are being observed by others who will judge them negatively. This contributes to the self-consciousness they experience in public.

That they often feel judged and criticized contributes to their feeling that they are not good enough or inferior to others. They will often not want to put too much focus on themselves or appear as though they are "showy" or egotistical.

Clinginess, weakness, and dependence are all traits that they don't want anyone else to notice about them, so they become very self-conscious when talking in groups, meeting someone new, or being assertive with those that are close to them. They will often try to present themselves as independent and strong individuals even if the reverse is true.

While it seems contradictory, these individuals may also seem very open or friendly and not self-conscious when talking with other members of their family or close friends. They can be outgoing and social in these situations but have a hard time being assertive at work. They tend to be self-critical and avoid making eye contact because they do not want others to see how anxious they are. Either way, this personality type easily gets embarrassed in public or with those that are close to them and they fear social rejection.

5. Difficulty or Refusal to Ask for Help

Many fearful avoidant individuals will avoid asking others for help when they need it. They will be reluctant to reach out for what they need as they worry about being rejected or that others won't like them. Some of them get so anxious about having to ask others for anything that it creates a sense of shame and despair.

They are often very self-reliant and independent. They tend to believe that they must learn how to handle life's challenges on their own. As a result, many fearful avoidant individuals always seem to be struggling in life. They always seem overwhelmed and unable to get their work done. They cannot seem to ask others for help and may feel that they are a burden on others or simply too "stupid" or inept. They may have difficulty admitting their weaknesses or apologizing for mistakes or failures because they believe this will make them look "weak."

When fearful avoidant individuals do admit that they need help, it can make them feel weak and unable to care for themselves. They fear the negative judgments of others in this situation. This can be frustrating and cause them to become angry or resentful. They frequently don't ask for assistance because they are too preoccupied with what others will think of them This goes back to the fear of being judged and rejected by someone else, especially in a professional environment.

6. Inability to Express Feelings

Individuals with a fearful avoidant personality type also have a very difficult time expressing their feelings. This can be especially challenging when they are dating or involved in close and intimate relationships with other individuals.

Fearful avoidant individuals may not express their anger or sadness because they worry about being rejected by others. They may even obsess over the anger and sadness they keep bottled up inside instead of expressing it to someone who might be able to help them deal with it. They have difficulty recognizing their feelings because of this fear and the distrust they have of others.

Underneath all their efforts to be seen as independent and strong individuals, some fearful avoidant individuals do want to seek out the support of others in some situations. They are afraid of being judged as weak or dependent and will only allow themselves to trust others when they feel that what they say is good enough or will lead them to success in life.

7. Strongly Antipathic to Anything or Anyone New or Different

Many fearful avoidant individuals have difficulty establishing healthy relationships because they fear rejection. They fear getting too close to someone else and feeling vulnerable. They remain alert because they worry about being rejected by others. They may find reasons not to interact with others so they don't have to worry about receiving feedback or judgment for their choices. This can cause problems for them in their social interactions and make them feel isolated.

8. Excessive Preoccupation with Success and Prestige

Fearful avoidants often place a great deal of importance on what they have accomplished in life, rather than keeping their attention on their feelings, needs, or interests. They are also often preoccupied with competition and performance. These individuals never feel as though they get enough attention or recognition for their actions because their insecurities about these issues keep them continually striving for more success.

Fearful avoidant individuals can become extremely competitive at times, and overly critical of themselves. This can make them self-conscious and anxious about getting into social situations with others, especially intimate ones.

Thanks to the fear of being criticized and rejected by others, these individuals tend to not trust others or any advice they might offer them that will help them improve their lives. They may become overly skeptical and distrustful and fearful of getting close to anyone in a way that could destroy their self-image as a strong, independent person.

9. Trends Toward Self-Destruction/Suicide

These individuals often feel very helpless and powerless. They frequently have very little respect for themselves and believe that their lives are not worthwhile. They may feel that there is nothing that they can do to change these feelings because they are so deeply affected by them.

Some fearful avoidant individuals may also experience severe panic attacks, which can cause them to believe that the world is going crazy around them. Because of this, some of these individuals may decide that life no longer has any meaning for them and become suicidal.

10. High Stress Threshold

These individuals often appear to be very resilient in the face of stress, which can make them appear to be calm and happy even when they are not. They often think that they can handle any situation in life because of their ability to control their thoughts and feelings.

While this is true for some of these individuals, most of the time, it is not. They may experience massive amounts of anxiety, panic attacks, or other adverse effects from stress. They will often be overly anxious and fearful of many social situations and public places, which can cause them to avoid any situation that might bring their anxiety up too high. When forced to interact with others for an extended period of time, this can make them seem icy and rude.

These characteristics can help explain why fearful avoidant individuals seem cold and uncaring when in reality they are very caring and sensitive. Because of the abuse and neglect, they have endured throughout their lives, the majority of them are frequently incredibly compassionate and caring individuals who have become emotionally numb. This causes them to become incapable of experiencing the same levels of love and affection for others that most people do.

CHAPTER 3

WHAT CAUSES FEARFUL AVOIDANT ATTACHMENT?

As stated in Chapter 1, a child's attachment style is formed through the bond that builds between themselves and their caregivers. The fearful avoidant attachment style occurs in about 7% of the population and typically develops in the first 18 months of life. Although it can happen later in childhood or adulthood, this usually isn't as severe as early attachment styles.

Fearful avoidant attachment is a complex issue often associated with several causes.

The following are several factors that play a part in the development of fearful avoidant attachment:

1. Genetics

Some children with fearful avoidant attachment are born with a genetic predisposition toward developing this attachment style. According to a National Institute of Mental Health study from 2010, there is a strong link between those who develop this attachment style and a specific genetic mutation that makes them anxious when they are alone.

The specific genes that can lead to fearful avoidant attachment are the oxytocin receptor gene (OXTR), brain-derived neurotrophic factor (BDNF), serotonin transporter gene (SERT), and the vasopressin transporter gene (AVPR1A), which accelerates the replication of the AVPR1A gene. The BDNF gene is known to affect communication between the nervous system and the brain. It also affects how busy that area of the brain is throughout a person's life. With a high BDNF gene, the nervous system will be very busy, which can lead to anxious feelings and hypervigilance in many situations. Other signs and symptoms linked to this gene include aggression, social anxiety, and depression.

Jocelynne Smith-Hayat (2010) found that the vasopressin transporter gene (AVPR1A) regulates the water supply to each brain region. This is known as osmolality. An excess of vasopressin in certain neurons will lead to a decrease in water transport and an increase in osmolality within those specific neurons, which can result in that neuron firing more often and can increase anxiety levels. Aggression and violent behavior, as well as anxiety disorders and depression, are some of the other symptoms linked to this gene.

The Serotonin Transporter Gene (SERT) helps regulate the brain's serotonin levels. A theory suggests that someone with a lower amount of serotonin is more likely to develop an avoidant attachment style. In these cases, they tend to feel isolated and detached from others, developing an independent and fearful personality later in life. According to studies, someone with lower levels of SERT is less likely to develop secure attachments with others.

Like BDNF, the AVPR1A gene also affects how busy the brain is. The AVPR1A gene helps regulate the water supply to each brain region. An excess of this substance causes a decrease in water transport within certain neurons and an increase in osmolality, which can increase anxiety levels. As a result of these differences in gene regulation, someone who has lower levels of AVPR1A is more likely to experience anxious feelings later in life and is also less likely to form secure attachments with their caregivers as adults.

There is a strong correlation between all three genes (OXTR, BDNF, and AVPR1A) and fearful attachment. These three genetic mutations interfere with the normal development of the brain and can lead to anxious feelings or depression later on in life. The National Institute of Mental Health study noted a strong connection between these genes and fearful attachment, depression, and other types of anxiety disorders.

2. Environmental Factors

Many environmental factors can lead to the development of fearful avoidant attachment in adulthood.

Some of the environmental factors that have been shown to cause fearful avoidant attachment include:

a. Childhood Abuse & Neglect

Empirical data has shown a strong correlation between childhood abuse and fearful attachment. Child abuse doesn't only refer to physical abuse; it can also refer to verbal abuse, emotional abuse, sexual abuse, and neglect. Studies have shown that over 60% of people who were abused or neglected as children were also shown to develop a fearful attachment style at some point in their life.

According to the DSM-IV, which was published in 2000 by the American Psychiatric Association, emotional neglect occurs when a parent fails to "provide emotional support for their child." In these cases, the parent is often unable to provide the child with comfort them when distressed; this can cause someone to internalize their feelings and become more withdrawn. DSM-IV is a widely accepted diagnostic manual currently in its fourth edition. Many mental health professionals use this manual to diagnose patients.

The National Institute of Mental Health (2010) states that children who grow up in an environment where they are not comforted by their parents or shown love and affection are more likely to develop fearful attachment patterns. In these cases, someone might feel overcome with fear when they try to form new connections or relationships out into the world as an adult.

b. Parental Alienation

Parents are supposed to be their child's protectors. To do that, however, the parent needs to take an interest in them and show them love and affection. This can prevent the children from developing fearful attachment styles later in life.

Several studies indicate that parental alienation can cause a child to develop fearful attachment patterns. In these instances, children might believe that their parent doesn't love or care about them, which can lead to a strong sense of rejection and abandonment. As a result of this rejection, the child feels frightened to form relationships with others and might feel like they don't have anyone they can rely on or trust.

According to the DSM-IV, one type of parental alienation is one parent refuses to have a relationship with the other parent. In some instances, the child may be forced to choose a side and make statements or comments against the other parent. When this happens, they feel like they can't rely on anyone else and may feel separated from others.

Other types of parental alienation include when one parent tries to control every aspect of their child's life, refuses to acknowledge that the other parent has a bond with them, causes their children to tell lies about the other parent, and/or refuses to allow contact with the other parent. These actions can have a very strong effect on the child and cause them to feel fearful and incapable of trusting others when they grow up.

c. Lack of Consistent Caregivers

Trusting others is something that is learned at a very young age. Children need to learn how to trust others to form relationships and bonds with them, according to the National Institute of Mental Health (2006). However, it can be difficult for a child to do that if they don't have anyone they can rely on upon consistently or form an attachment with.

Numerous studies demonstrate that someone who receives inconsistent care is more likely to develop a fearful avoidant attachment style. This can also include being left to their own devices or living with caregivers who care more about themselves than their children.

In a 2020 study, the National Institute of Mental Health concluded that a someone's environment contributes to their fear of intimacy. Researchers found that when the surrounding environment differed from how the individuals had been brought up, the children were more likely to develop fearful attachment styles.

Researchers at the University of California conducted another study in 2010. They found a direct correlation between attachment style and uncertainty about level of love. Researchers found that those who were not exposed to enough affection from their parents as children were more likely to develop fearful attachment styles.

d. Parental Conflict & Divorce

When parents are involved in a high level of conflict, they must make an effort to communicate with each other and resolve the issues they are having. If they don't, the stress of dealing with these issues can cause their children to become fearful and avoidant. The National Institute of Mental Health reported in 2010 that the greater the relationship conflict, the stronger the avoidant attachment style.

According to studies, children who experience their parents' conflict and distress as they grow up are more likely to later adopt fearful attachment styles. In these cases, they feel frightened and apprehensive about forming relationships with others as adults.

According to the DSM-IV, parental conflict occurs when parents fail to resolve their issues in a way that allows them to work together as a team. This is known as "marital discord" and can cause a child to feel fearful of rejection and abandonment.

In 2018, Jana Rosewarne, Ph.D., and Ollie Burrows published an article in the *Journal of Differential Psychology*. This article examined whether children who lived through their parents' separation had different attachment styles than those who did not. They looked at three groups of participants: children with fearful avoidant attachments, secure attachments, and those with insecure ambivalent attachments. The results showed that the insecure ambivalent group had the highest rate of living through parental separation. The authors concluded that these people developed the most issues when interacting with others as adults.

e. Sexual Abuse

A serious problem that has existed throughout history and that can harm children is child sexual abuse. Children who experience childhood sexual abuse are at risk of developing fearful avoidant attachments later in life, the National Institute of Mental Health stated in 2010.

In 2011, researchers at the University of Maryland Medical Center found that those who experienced these violent events had a greater chance of forming a fearful attachment style as an adult than those who had not been abused.

Other Factors

As fearful avoidant attachment can also occur later in childhood or adulthood, here are some things that can contribute to developing the disorder:

1. Mental Illness

Mental disorders can also cause one to develop a fearful avoidant attachment style. These may include:

a. Passive-aggressive Personality

Someone with a passive-aggressive personality is typically passive and nonconfrontational in their outward behavior. However, they tend to express their anger and discontent towards others through aggressive actions or stubbornness. These actions are usually directed toward those closest to them in their lives.

A study in 2018 by Bobbi J. Carothers and James E. Stinson, two doctors at the University of Central Arkansas, found a correlation between passive-aggressive personality traits and avoidant attachment styles later in life. This particular study was based on the Adult Attachment Inventory developed by Mary Ainsworth in 1978. Around 80% of those with avoidant attachment styles had passive-aggressive personality traits.

b. Borderline Personality Disorder

Borderline personality disorder (BPD) patients struggle with emotional and behavioral regulation. They are often very sensitive and impulsive, which can cause them to act inappropriately. For example, if they feel threatened or experience rejection, they might react by lashing out verbally or becoming physically aggressive.

Someone with BPD is usually very dependent on others. This dependency can make it difficult for them to construct relationships or cope after experiencing a significant loss or failure. These challenges can cause them to develop a fearful avoidant attachment style as an adult.

According to research published in the *American Journal of Psychiatry*, fearful avoidants have been found to have a higher chance of developing BPD. This is because they tend to be very dependent on others and are prone to breaking down in their life. They also have difficulty separating from others and form intense, passionate relationships characterized by instability or violence. Around 15% of people with BPD have a fearful avoidant attachment style.

c. Post-traumatic Stress Disorder

People with post-traumatic stress disorder (PTSD) experience severe anxiety when exposed to events that remind them of their traumatic past. They may experience flashbacks, uncontrollable thoughts, and nightmares. They often find it difficult to function normally and build relationships because of this fear.

Numerous studies have found that fearful avoidant attachment styles are typically associated with PTSD. Two medical professionals from University College London—Chris Bateman and Esther Klap—developed a model to explain why this kind of attachment is linked to PTSD in a study that was published in 2019 by the *Journal of Personality and Social Psychology*. According to the study, someone who has been through a traumatic experience is more likely to develop a fearful or avoidant attachment style due to a lack of trust in others. They will assume that others are not trustworthy and fail to form intimate relationships during their life. Around 30% of people with PTSD have fearful attachments.

d. Social Anxiety Disorder

People with a social anxiety disorder (SAD) have a high degree of anxiety in social situations. They might experience anxiety when they speak in front of others, participate in public speaking, or meet someone new. They are more likely to form close relationships with others who have the same traits.

A 2015 study published in the *Journal of Personality and Individual Differences* found that fearful avoidants were more likely to experience social anxiety disorders. This is because they have a high degree of insecurity and low self-confidence, which can make it difficult for them to develop close relationships with others. The study also found that women are more likely than men to develop this attachment style.

e. Body Dysmorphic Disorder

Someone with body dysmorphic disorder (BDD) worries a lot about how they look and how they think others see them. They cannot see themselves realistically, and they might obsess over their imaginary imperfections. People with this disorder are often preoccupied with their appearance, and they can spend excessive amounts of time checking on it or trying to alter it. They might engage in compulsive behaviors to change their appearance, such as excessive skin picking or dermatologic procedures (such as plastic surgery).

They might be afraid of rejection by others because of their appearance and may take defensive actions in an attempt to separate themselves from others. individuals. This can cause them to avoid social interactions with others.

BDD is associated with fearful or avoidant attachment styles, according to a 2015 study published in the *Journal of Anxiety Disorders*, because it makes someone dependent on themselves instead of others. Someone might develop a fearful attachment style because they assume that others will reject them based on their appearance. Approximately 50% of people with BDD have an avoidant attachment style.

2. Traumatic Injuries

Traumatic injuries can also cause fearful avoidant attachment styles. These include:

a. TBI

Traumatic brain injuries (TBIs) are caused by external forces such as crushing, penetrating, or shaking that can damage the brain and lead to neurological impairments. According to a study published in 2018 by *Frontiers in Behavioral Neuroscience*, someone with a TBI may have a fearful avoidant attachment style because of the feelings of insecurity, fear, and anxiety that occur during recovery. This can cause these individuals to withdraw from social interactions and affect their ability to form intimate relationships Studies have found that around 20% of people with a TBI develop an avoidant attachment style because of these anxieties.

b. Stroke

The interruption of blood flow that leads to brain damage is the cause of a stroke. According to a study published by the

Brain and Behavior Journal (2016), someone who has suffered a stroke can have a fearful avoidant attachment style because of their feelings of insecurity, fear, and anxiety. The anxiety that results from the injury can cause these individuals to withdraw from social interaction. Studies have found that around 19% of stroke victims develop an avoidant attachment style because of these anxieties.

c. Brain Tumors

Brain tumors can cause harm to the brain and neurological functions by interfering with normal cellular functioning. According to a 2017 study published by *Current Neurology & Neuroscience Reports*, someone with a brain tumor may have an avoidant fearful attachment style due to feelings of insecurity, fear, and anxiety. Studies have found that around 26% percent of people with a brain tumor develop an avoidant attachment style because of this anxiety.

Brain tumors often lead to neurological impairments that make it hard to maintain normal relationships. In addition, these impairments changes how someone perceive themselves and others, making it difficult for them to establish healthy attachments.

d. Autoimmune Diseases

When the immune system attacks healthy cells, an autoimmune condition develops. *Brain and Behavior* published a study in 2017 indicating that someone with an autoimmune disease may have a fearful avoidant attachment style due to feelings of insecurity, fear, and anxiety. Studies have found that around 30% of people with an autoimmune disease develop an avoidant attachment style because of these anxieties.

3. Chemical Imbalances

A chemical imbalance is a condition in which the body's chemistry does not have the right balance of neurotransmitters such as serotonin, dopamine, and norepinephrine. Serotonin sends signals between nerve cells in the brain and contributes to feelings of happiness and well-being. Dopamine controls behavior and feelings. Norepinephrine alerts the body to danger or stressful situations. A chemical imbalance can cause several problems within the body and can lead to several different disorders.

Those with serotonin imbalance often feel an increase in anxiety, depression, and irritability. They also might experience mood swings and feel an increase in anger or hostility. Those with a dopamine imbalance often feel increased aggression, hyperactivity, and impulsiveness. They may also require treatment for hallucinations or delusions, and may feel confused or disoriented when trying to think clearly.

One study found that having a chemical imbalance can cause someone to develop an avoidant attachment style because of the increased feelings of insecurity that result from their condition. They often feel fearful and anxious about their condition because they have no control over what is happening in their bodies.

According to a study published in 2015 by *Current Psychiatry Reviews*, those with a chemical imbalance can have a fearful avoidant attachment because of their insecurity and fear.

4. Drug Use

Drug addiction can cause avoidant attachment because of the feelings of insecurity, fear, and anxiety it causes. Turning to drugs can cause someone to feel angry or hostile, leading them to develop an anxious fearful attachment style because of their feelings of insecurity, fear, and anxiety.

Many people who lack personal relationships or have unhealthy relationships with others turn to drugs and alcohol to cope with their feelings. These coping methods can cause avoidant attachment styles because they prevent someone from forming close relationships. Due to their preoccupation with obtaining their next dose of substances, they frequently fail to form healthy friendships or intimate relationships. Therefore, substance abusers begin to turn away from others and become more independent, making it difficult for them to develop healthy intimate relationships.

Following stressful life events such as divorce or the death of a family member, approximately 64% of participants in one study reported turning to drugs for comfort. These events often cause them to feel insecure and anxious, making it difficult for them to develop intimate relationships.

5. Low IQ

According to research, individuals with a lower IQ are more likely to develop an avoidant attachment style. This is because they might not be able to express themselves to get what they need from others properly. As a result, they become frustrated with those around them and avoid seeking assistance when it would be beneficial.

Men and women who score below 80 on a standardized intelligence test are considered intellectually disabled. One study found that someone with an intellectual disability is more likely to develop an avoidant attachment style than those who score above 80. This study found that a low IQ makes it difficult for individuals to "understand the intentions and actions of others in close relationships" and is a risk factor for fearful avoidant attachment.

The CDC indicates that approximately 1 in 4 people with an intellectual disability struggle with social skills and interpersonal relationships. Studies suggest that this is because they might not understand what love means or what being in a relationship requires. In addition, these individuals might struggle with communicating their feelings, which makes it difficult for them to get the support they need. This can cause them to feel very insecure and can lead to a fearful avoidant attachment style later on in life.

6. Loss of a Loved One

It can be hard to accept a loved one's death. As a result, there might be many weeks (or months) before someone feels able to start grieving for their deceased family member or friend. When these feelings of grief begin to surface, it can cause them to develop a fearful avoidant attachment style.

People will often fear experiencing the same kind of loss in the future. They might be reluctant to start new relationships or put more energy into existing ones. This can cause their relationships to become more unstable, eventually leading to their social circle becoming very small.

There may be higher risks when someone has a fearful avoidant attachment style and is going through a lot of grief after losing a loved one. Some people who have suffered a loss might feel like they cannot properly grieve or cope with their emotions. This can lead to an ongoing negative cycle that prevents them from fully accepting their loved one's death.

6. Brain Damage from Lack of Oxygen During Birth

The American Red Cross states that if there is insufficient oxygen in the womb to support brain development, a child could experience different birth defects or even structural brain damage. This may cause them to develop a fearful avoidant attachment style.

Being born prematurely can also cause defects in the brain. These birth defects are caused when the baby is not developed in a way that allows them to have normal control of their breath. Less than 5% of premature babies are born without any brain or organ damage. These babies are at high risk of developing structural abnormalities. For example, some children born prematurely have been found to have smaller brains later on in life, and they might be even more anxious than others.

The risk of having a fearful avoidant attachment is increased because they might not grow up with the same neural connections required for a secure attachment style.

7. Sleep deprivation

Those with volatile sleep schedules or who are constantly overworked can suffer from sleep deprivation. In the long run, this can wear them down emotionally and physically, which can cause them to develop a fearful avoidant attachment style, according to the National Institute of Mental Health (2010). If a person doesn't get enough sleep, it may be difficult for them to concentrate on their daily tasks. They often have trouble attaining a sense of calmness and security in their lives.

Sleep deprivation can also have a direct effect on relationships. They often have difficulty getting close to others. They do not even get the basic essentials that they need to support their health and well-being. For example, someone who has trouble sleeping might not be able to go to the gym or talk to a therapist to reduce stress. This can make them unattractive candidates for long-term relationships or friendships that last into adulthood.

The National Sleep Foundation reports that people need about eight hours of sleep per night to function properly, but most adults worldwide are sleeping less than this. Those who don't get enough sleep may feel drained and irritable. This can cause them to act more defensively around others and behave in less cooperative and encouraging ways. As a result, they might be viewed as more anxious, afraid, insecure, and avoidant of others throughout their lives.

For good physical and mental health, sleep is necessary. The National Heart, Lung and Blood Institute (NHLBI) published a scientific statement in 2010 which indicates that with the right kind of sleep, people can have better focus and self-regulation throughout the day. The NHLBI points out that although good sleep habits might not be able to eliminate all negative thoughts, they can help someone feel more at ease in their everyday lives.

There are many causes of a fearful avoidant attachment style. Having a fearful avoidant attachment style does not mean that you are incapable or unintelligent. It simply indicates that you do not understand the intentions and actions of others, which can cause you to feel fearful, anxious, or insecure in social situations.

PART 2

FEARFUL AVOIDANTS IN RELATIONSHIPS

CHAPTER 4

HOW FEARFUL AVOIDANTS LOVE

Love is a strong emotion that has the ability to unite or divide people. When someone with fearful avoidant attachment loves, it can either be a blessing or a disaster. This is because this is a complicated attachment style that involves strong feelings of love, fear, and anxiety.

Characteristics of Someone with a Fearful Avoidant Attachment

The following are some of the main characteristics of fearful avoidant attachment in relationships:

1. Obsession

Fearful avoidants are generally very dependent on their relationships. In relationships, they can become obsessed with the status of their partner. They will focus heavily on their partner and how they feel, even when it is inappropriate. They will often wonder how their partner feels or whether they are confused about something.

Fearful avoidants who are not in a relationship will often be obsessed with the idea of being in a relationship, often to the point where they think about nothing else. They tend to be emotionally dependent and crave companionship. They want to feel needed and are frightened that no one will ever love them. Fearful avoidants with this attachment style can find it difficult to let go when a relationship ends, even if they were in the wrong relationship.

2. Intense Love

Fearful avoidants will sometimes obsess over a potential partner and their feelings of love. This can provoke intense anxiety if doubts start circling in their head. If their partner ignores them, walks away, or puts space between them, their heart is broken, and they feel devastated. They go through emotions of frustration, anger, hurt, and sadness.

Fearful avoidants with this attachment style are strongly influenced by their emotions and often ignore facts. They tend to make decisions based on how they feel at the time, without thinking things through in advance. This frequently results in them making poor decisions.

3. Jealousy

Fearful avoidants can get very jealous. They are very possessive and will often try to gain control over their partner by determining how they think, feel and act. This can sometimes make them appear as though they do not trust their partner, which can cause problems in the relationship. A relationship needs to allow for the expression and sharing of emotions by both parties. However, if someone feels they have no right to tell someone how they should feel, this can lead to jealousy and possessiveness in a fearful avoidant.

Fearful avoidants generally want to keep an eye on their partner, wanting to know where they have been and who they have been with. Sometimes, fearful avoidants will accuse their partners of having affairs or cheating on them when there has not been any evidence of this at all.

4. Egocentricity

Fearful avoidants have a natural tendency to put themselves first. They feel they are more important than everyone else and have a strong sense of entitlement. They think what they want should be the most important thing in the world. Those in relationships tend to be egocentric and may not think about what someone else wants from them because they are so focused on themselves. This can lead to them believing that their feelings are more important than those of others.

5. Avoidance

Most fearful avoidants do not like being touched by others. They will often avoid physical contact and are not very affectionate. They are afraid of being rejected and of letting someone in. They have a hard time depending on others and tend to have a "hold-off" attitude when it comes to physical touch.

Fearful avoidants in romantic relationships are often afraid of intimacy because they fear the pain of being left by their partner or the possibility that their partner will lose interest in them. They often keep their relationship at a distance because they do not want to feel close to someone in case the other party is not interested in them.

There are a few reasons why fearful avoidants have trouble with physical contact. The first reason is that they may have experienced hurt and loss in the past and are scared of giving their heart to someone else who might break it. They may have experienced unrequited love or even rejection from previous partners. This can make them feel that getting close to someone else is pointless because it will never work out, and so there is no point in trying. They also do not want to rely on others because they are afraid of being hurt by them. Someone in the past has hurt them, so they do not want to risk it happening again.

6. Disorganized Thinking

Fearful avoidants often have very disorganized thinking. They do not worry about big problems that most people think about, such as losing their job or moving house. They are not very good at taking the time to look at their problems and thinking about them logically. They are usually worrying about something that is happening right now and have a hard time looking ahead. This causes them to get angry, annoyed, or frustrated very easily.

Fearful avoidants may worry a lot about their partner's past relationships or even the future of their relationship. They might think that their partnership is bad for them or worry that there will be problems in the future because they do not feel they can solve them. They tend to speak in an extreme way and will use words like "always" and "never."

7. Insecurity

Fearful avoidants have a lot of insecurities and have a hard time with criticism. They are very sensitive to what others say about them and will often worry about how they are perceived. They may even feel that everyone is out to get them or to judge them because they are not perfect.

They may think that someone will use their past against them and that their partner will not want to be with them anymore. Overwhelming fear has caused their self-esteem to go down, making them even more angry, upset and worried, making them feel even more insecure and worried.

8. Defensive Strategies

Fearful avoidants will often retreat from their partner or the situation if they are feeling insecure because of their past. They will often believe that their partner is out to get them or do something bad to them. When someone avoids a situation like this because they feel they will not be able to solve it or be able to handle what others say, this is called "retreating," which is the defensive strategy of fearful avoidants.

This withdrawal from the situation makes it hard for the fearful avoidant to communicate with their partner and solve problems when they come up. They struggle to resolve the problem at hand because they are afraid of being rejected and receiving criticism. As a result, they become defensive when there is a problem. This causes stress for both partners.

Fearful avoidants will try to escape the situation if they feel they cannot handle what is happening. This can make it hard for a solution to be reached. When this happens, both parties may begin to show anger or defensive tendencies.

9. Avoiding Risky Situations

Fearful avoidants often have trouble taking risks and experiencing new things in life because they have a lot of fear or anxiety. This fear can cause a lot of anxiety because it makes them believe that others may not approve of what they are doing and how alone and uncomfortable they will feel if their partner does not agree with them.

This fear can cause depression and other mental issues. They may feel as though it is useless to put themselves out there. This can cause loneliness and antisocial behavior.

10. Compliance with Authority

Fearful avoidants will often comply with the rules established by authorities because they feel it will keep them safe. They may also not want to do anything dangerous because of how uncomfortable it makes them feel. This can make them timid and compliant. Since they are afraid of others rejecting them, they will often follow the rules.

11. Reactivity, Perfectionism, Self-doubt, and Dependency

Behaviors driven by fear usually occur out of a dysfunctional way of thinking. Many times this dysfunctional thinking is set in place because of how they were raised. This makes it hard for fearful avoidants to see how their behavior impacts those around them.

The fearful avoidant may see themselves as having to be perfect in everything they do, which leaves them with little time to relax.

12. Unconscious Fears

A sense of vulnerability can cause a fearful avoidants to become inflexible in their thoughts and actions. They begin to push their partners away when they try to work out any problems or issues they may be having. This may make them seem distant.

They will often blame their partner for problems that arise during their relationship, which can cause both of them to become defensive and angry. They will not be able to communicate with their partner without feeling insecure. They may try to control the relationship in an attempt to make sure that they do not get hurt again.

13. Overgeneralization

The fearful avoidant is usually hypervigilant of their partner's actions and will often make over-generalizations about their partner. This leads them to believe that the other party is harming them. They display a high level of distrust and think that everyone is out to get them and that nothing can be done to make them feel safe in their own lives. This can lead them to end up in unhealthy relationships because of how much harm they believe will come to them if they do not take precautions. They tend to see the world as a scary place and will often go out of their way to avoid any potential harm coming to them. This can have a negative emotional impact on both themselves and others.

CHAPTER 5

HOW FEARFUL AVOIDANTS BREAK UP

Relationships with someone with fearful avoidant attachment often lead to break-ups. Love is not easy. When people love each other, we have to go through many difficulties. But relationships with fearful avoidants are much more complicated than regular relationships. The fearful avoidant attachment can be very hard to understand. Even when they try to understand their partner, they might fail and make many mistakes. This may result in their break-up or separation.

How Fearful Avoidants Deals With Break-Ups

A reaction to breakup for fearful avoidants is generally very different from what others might experience. The following reactions are considered normal:

1. Shock and Denial

When a relationship ends for someone with fearful avoidant attachment, they often feel shocked and unable to process what is happening. They feel as though their entire world has come to an end, and that their partner has betrayed them in some way. They will be very disappointed in their partner, and they will believe that the relationship was not meant to last. Still, it is the expectations that the person had of their partner that caused the problem in the first place. They expected perfection from their partner and did not get what they wanted.

2. Lingering Neediness

Someone with a fearful attachment is afraid that they might not find someone as good as their ex was, so they feel very sad to lose them. They feel a lot of despair. This sadness will linger in them for a long time. They are often afraid that they might never feel good again. In time, they will be able to move on with their life, but it will never be easy for them.

3. Anger and Resentment

Fearful avoidants tend to become very angry at those who broke up with them, but what they do not realize is that it is because of their fear that things did work out between them. They feel as if their lives have been shattered and that everything has gone wrong. When people are overcome by internal emotions, they often overreact to situations and make them worse than they already are.

Someone with a fearful avoidant attachment will typically feel resentful toward their ex-partner after a breakup, and they won't be able to think straight. They do not want to start over with someone different, so they get stuck in a lot of anger and resentment. While it is normal to experience this anger, they need to talk about their feelings with someone who will understand where they are coming from but also help them see how things have gone wrong.

4. Avoidance of Anything Related to the Ex

Fearful avoidants need time to themselves to deal with all the emotions they are feeling, and it is normal for them to be afraid of anything that might remind them of their former partner. They are afraid that they might see something or someone who will make them think about the past and cause them to start feeling sad again, so it is easier for them not to go out and do the things that they like.

They will avoid anything that might be linked with those who broke up with them, including things that remind them of the good times. They might wonder why it did not work out with their ex and start feeling sad again, so avoiding these memories can prevent them feeling sorry for themselves or getting over something they know they should have been able to get over a long time ago.

5. Avoidance of Other Relationships

After ending a relationship with someone that was supposed to be their "soulmate," fearful avoidants do not want to think about the future and only want to live in the present moment. They are often afraid of getting into another relationship. When they think about trying again, it makes them feel as if this is not something that will make them happy anymore.

6. Rebound Relationships

Someone afraid of getting hurt emotionally will try to move on as soon as possible, but the problem is that someone who has been in a relationship for a long time should not move on so quickly. Nonetheless, they may rush into another relationship because they do not want to let it pass them by.

7. Retreat Into a Fantasy World

Fearful avoidants are afraid of getting hurt, so it makes sense that they avoid things that remind them of how their ex hurt them in the past. They often retreat into a fantasy world where no one hurts them, and they are always safe, even if this is not how things are in real life.

8. Self-Destructive Behavior

Fearful avoidants might start abusing drugs or alcohol to avoid the pain, even though it is clear that this is not healthy. They start drinking or doing drugs to avoid thinking about how their ex left them, and how nothing in their lives will ever be good again. They need to stop being self-destructive and try something new instead.

9. Going to Clubs and Hitting On the Wrong People

Fearful avoidants might hit on the wrong person when they are out at a club. This is a normal part of getting over someone, but it can be hard for fearful avoidants to figure out what is right or wrong when dating again after their ex breaks up with them. This can lead to them dating the wrong type of a person, and they might get hurt.

10. Severe Depression

Fearful avoidants may find it difficult to move on after a break-up because they feel alone in the world. They might be able to move on from this if they believe that others care about them and will never hurt them, but if they do not think this way, there is no way that they will ever get over being dumped. It can cause them to feel severely depressed.

11. Negative Anticipation

After a breakup, a fearful avoidant might find that they only want to get into another relationship to make things better, but this means that they will be going after a new relationship even though they are nervous about what will happen. They want to make sure that this new relationship does not end badly.

This is where they prepare for the worse, and all of the anticipations around having a broken heart make them have a hard time moving on from the past.

12. Self-Indulgence

Another way that fearful avoidants can react to their breakup is by indulging in things they know they should not be doing. They feel they deserve to be loved because they are loyal. They feel their partner should love them, but the relationship is a disaster. When the relationship ends, it feels very personal and painful. They know that this failure is something that they need to deal with, but they also want to feel special, and they want those who hurt them to feel bad about what happened.

Fearful avoidants can be very different from one another in how they deal with their relationships ending. Some might be fine with it, but others will want to keep returning and reliving the past. The last thing that anyone wants is for someone to be in this kind of pain, and it is best to make sure that you never get into a relationship with someone who has fearful avoidant attachment.

Overall, fearful avoidant attachment is something that should not be taken lightly. It can be very hard on those experiencing it because they do not know how to handle being hurt by the someone they love. The various emotions that result from love, pain, and heartbreak can be the hardest thing to get through. But this is something that can be dealt with.

CHAPTER 6

AM I FEARFUL AVOIDANT?

Now that you know the characteristics of someone with fearful avoidant attachment, it is now time to identify whether you may have this disorder yourself. Identifying whether you are a fearful avoidant will allow you to take the steps needed to start having great relationships.

Most of the time, fearful avoidants do not realize they have issues until they find themselves in emotionally intense situations or relationships where their fears keep them from having a healthy relationship with someone. At this point, something inside of them begins to recognize that there is more that needs to be done for them to have healthy relationships.

How to Determine If You Have a Fearful Avoidant Attachment Style

To identify whether you may be a fearful avoidant, it is important to determine whether you have the general attributes. These characteristics are very similar to the ones we have already covered. Answer affirmatively or negatively to determine if you belong to the category of fearful avoidant attachment.

You might have a fearful avoidant attachment if you provided a yes answer to at least five of the questions above. It is important to understand that not all of the questions need to be addressed for this pattern of behavior to qualify. The more yeses you gave, the more likely it is that you are a fearful avoidant.

The Fearful Avoidant Attachment Questionnaire

The F-AQ, also known as the Fearful Avoidance Questionnaire, is another way of determining whether you may have a fearful avoidant attachment. It was created to assess the relationship behaviors of someone with fearful avoidant attachment. It is a valid and reliable measurement tool that acts as a guide to help someone understand whether they have a fearful avoidant attachment or not. The F-AQ is a self-report scale-response format tool created by Dr. Thomas Armstrong in the U.K., in 1995. The F-AQ is administered very simply. To complete the tool, you have to answer all 33 questions on a scale from 0 to 4, where 0 is the least anxious, and 4 is the most anxious.

The higher the score is on the F-AQ, the more fearful avoidant you are. According to the test, a score of 81 or higher is considered high.

Now that you know whether or not you fit into the category of fear avoidant attachment, you are now in a much better position to make the changes needed to have happy and healthy relationships.

PART 3

OVERCOMING FEARFUL AVOIDANCE

CHAPTER 7

UNDERSTANDING MY TRIGGERS

The first step to overcoming your fearful avoidance is understanding what causes you to avoid certain situations or people. Knowing the triggers that cause your anxiety will help you to understand yourself better and develop coping strategies for those situations that you find most difficult.

Common Triggers of Someone with Fearful Avoidance Attachment

1. Criticism

Criticism and judgment are very common triggers for someone with fearful avoidant attachment. This is due to the fear of being judged or rejected due to their past experiences with criticism from their parents. They often judge themselves and try to avoid situations where they will be criticized or judged. They can react very hostilely when confronted with criticism and judgment from anyone close to them, including their partner.

Some ways they may react include:

a. Withdrawing and being more passive

Fearful avoidants may become more passive in the presence of criticism. This can create friction in a relationship and can cause both parties to feel frustrated and resentful toward one another.

b. Aggression and defensiveness

When someone with fearful avoidant attachment is criticized, they may react more aggressively and defensively than someone who has a secure attachment would. They may show intense anger and aggression towards their partner rather than listening to what they say or trying to work together on the issue that was brought up. This can cause the relationship to crumble very quickly, as it will create a lot of mistrust between both partners.

c. Blaming their partner

When faced with criticism from their partner, someone with a fearful avoidant attachment may think that it's their partner's fault for making them feel insecure or emotional. They may try to deflect any blame placed on them by blaming their partner instead.

Criticism and judgment are two of the most common triggers for fearful avoidants. They fear being judged or rejected, and they may react to it by turning away or completely withdrawing from their partner. This will create a lot of friction in the relationship, which can lead to both parties feeling very insecure and uncomfortable.

2. Disagreements and Arguments

Disagreements or arguments are one of the biggest triggers for someone with fearful avoidance. This is due to their lack of confidence. They are unwilling to put their partner through threatening situations because they lack faith in their capacity to do so. Conflict and disagreements with loved ones are avoided as a result. They quickly take the initiative to stop an argument or fight from starting.

This trigger can cause someone with fearful avoidance attachment to react in a number of ways that may not be appropriate, including:

a. Shouting and being overly aggressive

Shouting at someone is a way to express anger and frustration, and can be an indication of unresolved childhood t or emotional trauma. Their partner may feel threatened by the shouting and may become afraid, which causes more problems in the relationship.

b. Making snide comments or being sarcastic during arguments

Sarcasm is something that someone use to hide their insecurities. As they are being criticized, they are trying to deflect the attention away from themselves because they feel threatened by what is being said or fear that they will be judged.

c. Making excuses or using "red herrings"

A fearful avoidant may try to make an excuse or ask their partner a question to distract them so that their partner will not be able to form a rebuttal or an explanation. This is meant to deflect the criticism away from them. In the end, though, it causes resentment where they might have been able to work through their issues with their partner had they not tried to avoid conflict in the first place.

d. Withdrawing from their partner

Sometimes, fearful avoidants will completely withdraw from their partner when they are in the middle of an argument or a disagreement. They may feel that it is better not to be around others in this situation, and they may become uncomfortable to the point where they want to get away from their partner altogether rather than tackle the issue at hand.

Fearful avoidants will often try to push their partner away from them when they feel angry by making snide comments, repeating the same sentence over and over again, or becoming aggressive. This may seem like it is a way of being mean and hurtful, but it is just a way for them to cope with the situation. It has become a habit for them through years of conditioning.

3. Boredom

Fearful avoidants are often afraid of boredom, and they seek excitement to feel satisfied. Boredom often causes them to feel unsatisfied with their life, so they seek new things or experiences to fill the void.

Some ways that they may react when they are bored include:

a. Making a scene

Making a scene is an attention-grabbing behavior that they may have learned from their parents. It means that they want someone to notice them or look at them. They seek attention and excitement through these behaviors and want their partner to acknowledge the effort they put into the relationship. When their partner doesn't react the way they want, they may become angry and resentful.

b. Having an affair

They attempt to add interest to their lives by doing this, but in the long run, it might be more harmful than helpful. An affair is exciting for a fearful avoidant because it helps them feel excited about themselves again, but will obviously cause problems within the relationship.

c. Use alcohol or drugs

Fearful avoidants often use alcohol or drugs to fill the void that is present due to their dissatisfaction with themselves. This is a way for them to forget about their problems and unhappiness. This can cause serious problems in relationships because it can lead to attempts of suicide or controlling behaviors. When you are trying to fill the void through addictive substances, it can cause serious problems in your life.

d. Indulgence in dangerous activities

They often participate in reckless and dangerous activities to feel satisfied. This can include risky sports like boxing or wrestling, or driving while under the influence of alcohol or drugs. When they are participating in these activities, they don't feel bored.

e. Unhealthy sexual behavior

Fearful avoidants often engage in sexual behavior that is not healthy and is meant to fill the void they feel inside. This can involve engaging in promiscuous sexual behavior, unsafe sex, or having multiple partners just for the sake of having sex. Their partner may become extremely unhappy with this sort of situation.

4. Feeling Abandoned

Another thing that can trigger someone with a fearful avoidant attachment is feeling abandoned. If they feel their partner has abandoned them somehow, they can become angry and unforgiving. They might also become angrier if they believe their partner has let them down in some way.

Some ways that you can tell that a person is feeling abandoned are:

a. Distant behavior

Because they believe their partner has abandoned them, they may become angry and resentful. When someone with a fearful avoidant attachment, they are very scared that their partner will leave them or dump them for someone else. Similarly, if they feel their partner has let them down, they may try to control the situation. They may act jealous and angry and make threats or use less-than-positive remarks towards them.

This behavior is a way for them to fill the void of not feeling satisfied with themselves. It is also a way for them to get their partner to be more involved with them; when they feel as if their partner is not there for them, they become angry and resentful.

b. Defensiveness

This is another sign of feeling abandoned because when someone feels as though their partner has left them, they act out defensively. They may also become defensive when their partner tries to talk to them about what they are experiencing because they would rather feel like they have the upper hand in the situation.

This behavior is common in fearful avoidants because they are trying to find ways to feel more important. This causes problems in the relationship because it makes their partner feel upset, which can lead to serious disagreements.

c. Jealousy

Another sign of abandonment is when someone feels their partner is more interested in someone else. This behavior is common in fearful avoidants, who often fear that their partner does not want to be with them anymore.

d. Anger

When a fearful-avoidant believes their partner no longer cares about them because they have developed an interest in someone else, this can make them feel angry and resentful. They may try to keep a close eye on them, or they may try to be around them as much as possible to ensure their partner is not talking with anyone else.

This can also cause problems in their relationships because it makes their partner upset, which can lead to serious disagreements.

e. Noncompliance with demands

If you are in a relationship with a fearful avoidant, you may notice that they do not always comply with your demands, and they may get angry if you try to make them do something. They may also resent you because they feel you are controlling them and making demands on what they have to do or not do. This can cause a lot of tension in their relationship because they try to avoid you as much as possible because they do not like being told what to do. This can also cause problems in their relationships because of the lack of respect they show their partner, and can lead to serious disagreements.

5. Not Being in Control of a Situation

Not having control over a situation can also trigger fearful avoidant because they have insecurities about losing their partners to someone else. They fear that their partner will leave them for someone else, which makes them feel as though they will be alone in the world.

This can make them feel a range of emotions, including:

a. Scared and desperate

Not being able to control situations can also cause a fearful avoidant to feel scared and desperate because they do not know what their partner is thinking or planning. This can make them feel anger and resentment. They may also become scared or angry if they believe their partner may leave them without any reason or warning. This can cause serious problems in their relationship because it will make both of them feel angry and insecure, leading to serious disagreements between the two.

b. Destructive and crazy

Fearful avoidants may become extremely aggressive when they lack control. They may become angry and aggressively demanding towards their partner, making both of them feel scared and angry. This can cause serious problems in their relationship.

Lack of control over a situation can also make them feel extremely upset and as though they are completely in the hands of their partner. This can cause serious problems in their relationship.

c. Depressed

Having no control over a situation can also induce depression in fearful avoidants because they feel that they do not have a place to go and no one to depend on. They may feel guilty, upset, and depressed because they may believe they did something to earn their partner's lack of affection. They may also feel helpless because they believe there is nothing they can do to change the situation as their partner has already decided who they will be with in the future and has left them behind.

This makes them feel as though they are completely alone in the world and have no one to depend on. They may also feel that there is nothing they can do to save their relationship because their partner has been making decisions for them both. This can cause serious problems in the relationship because it makes both of them feel helpless and upset, leading to serious disagreements between the two.

d. Suicidal

Having no control over situations can also lead to suicidal thoughts in a fearful avoidant because they may feel there is nothing they can do to change their life. If their partner has left them or passed away, they may think it's pointless to continue living. As a result, they may become extremely insecure, depressed, and anxious.

e. Nervous

Feeling nervous is common with fearful avoidant attachment when a situation is out of control. It may make them feel apprehensive because they believe their partner will leave them for someone new without any warning or reason.

This trigger of having no control over a situation can cause serious problems in a relationship with someone with fearful-avoidant attachment because it makes the both of them to feel extremely anxious, upset, and depressed. The relationship may suffer because both parties will begin to believe that there is nothing they can do to prevent the end of their union.

6. Lack of Direction

Lack of direction in the relationship is also a trigger for someone with fearful-avoidant attachment because it causes them to feel as though there is no end goal in their relationship. They are never sure what is expected from them, and they will often meet their partner's needs by doing everything they ask. This spells disaster for the relationship, as when it comes to meeting their partner's needs, there is always a sense of "I can do better than that" inside most people. This puts pressure on both parties and can leave one or both partners frustrated with the relationship.

Some ways in which they may react to a lack of direction in a relationship are:

a. Withdrawing/passivity

Fearful avoidants will distance themselves from situations that make them anxious or concerned for a variety of reasons, including uncertainty about what to do or how to act or, in some cases, the belief that they are burdening their partner. They may think, "I don't want to create tension or an argument between us. It's easier for me if I keep quiet." So they withdraw instead of confronting their partner. This will make the relationship extremely tense, causing disagreement and animosity between them.

When someone is afraid to confront their partner or cause a problem in the relationship, they may react by becoming passive and withdrawing from their partner. This will cause serious problems in their relationship because it will make both parties feel trapped in the relationship because of fear and anxiety.

b. Being overly-submissive

In relationships with a fearful avoidant, there is often a sense that "you either have control over me and possess me, or you don't, and I'm not interested." This can lead to them being overly submissive in their relationship and pleasing their partner at all times. This can be harmful in relationships because it creates a situation in which their partner is never happy or satisfied with what they get, leading to them looking for satisfaction elsewhere.

c. Not complaining about things that are not going well in the relationship

If there is a problem in the relationship, then a fearful avoidant will be extremely reluctant to confront their partner about it, no matter how much they might want to. They feel as though they are always responsible for everything that happens in the relationship and that if they complain, then they will be blamed or blamed via guilt. If a problem arises and they do not speak up about it, their partner might end the relationship with them out of frustration. This will cause serious problems because this essentially means that one or both parties are escaping responsibility for problems and failures in their relationships, which will leave them feeling empty and sad about the situation.

d. Withholding affection/intimacy

Fearful avoidants will often withhold affection or intimacy from their partner to avoid being hurt. They may think, "I can't let myself forget I'm vulnerable. I have to make sure I always know that they still care about me. If I don't, I'll get extremely upset and hurt." So instead of showing their lover that they mean something to them, they will sometimes hold back to protect themselves. This can cause serious problems in the relationship because it will make them feel as though they are not needed by their partner and could leave at any time for someone new who does show them affection or care about them in a way that their partner doesn't.

e. Avoiding the situation when the other person wants to discuss their problems

Fearful avoidants avoid confrontation at all costs to avoid any sense of conflict between them and their partner. Instead of confronting their partner about problems in the relationship, they will usually do whatever they can to ignore or avoid them altogether. This can cause serious problems because their partner is not being helped when issues need to be brought up for the situation to improve. It can also lead to them feeling unloved or unwanted, leading to them withdrawing completely from the relationship.

The feeling of losing the direction in the relationship is a big trigger to the fearful-avoidant because it touches on the "fear of being a failure as a couple" and having to start over. This fear often manifests itself as the fear of being abandoned, which is where physical withdrawal becomes a possibility.

These are some of the triggers that fearful avoidant individuals feel, making it hard for them to make decisions in their relationships, express their feelings, and allow themselves to be vulnerable. You may have a partner or have been in a relationship with a fearful avoidant who can relate to these feelings or have heard of a partner's story. It is important to understand that everyone has different needs when it comes to relationships, and you should never feel like you "should" be doing something your partner wants if it doesn't make you happy.

Identifying Your Triggers

Finding the precise causes of your triggers can be challenging. This is especially true if you are a fearful avoidant or have ever been in a relationship with someone who is.

How to Identify Your Triggers

1. Journaling

An excellent way to express your thoughts and feelings about your significant other, your friends, and your family is through your journal. It will assist you in determining what you believe to be right and wrong in relation to the circumstances you are going through. You can determine if something, in particular is upsetting or worrying you by writing down your thoughts.

How can you do this?

Step 1: Write down all your thoughts

To identify your triggers through journaling, write down your thoughts and feelings concerning someone. Include any ideas about what you believe others are thinking when they are being distant or not listening to you. It can be a good way to observe how others live their lives and to understand what is causing them to be the way they are. You can also write down how you feel throughout the day or things that happen to you that make you feel a certain way. It could also be a good to write down your feelings about your partner or someone else close to you. You can also write down if something has happened to you that has caused you to feel different emotions than usual. It may be beneficial to journal only once or twice per week so you don't become overwhelmed or discouraged.

Step 2: Re-Read Your Journal

When it has been several days since you last wrote down everything in your journal, read it and look over what you have written. Try to find patterns in how you feel and think about things, as well as patterns in how others are treating you. Review your journal once a month to avoid becoming overwhelmed by the information you have recorded there.

Ask yourself questions and try to answer them honestly. Think about how you feel in certain situations, like when there are a lot of people around you, or when you are at work, school, or somewhere else, and you are left to your own devices.

Questions like:

- What am I avoiding?

-

What do other people do that makes me feel uncomfortable?

- If someone close to me didn't want to be around me all the time, what would it make me feel?

- Why do I feel that way?

- How would I describe the feelings that I get around someone?

- How does someone treat me differently when they are in a good mood and when they are in a bad mood?

In order to learn how to deal with similar circumstances in the future, you should also keep track of your worst experiences and pinpoint what led to them. By recording your thoughts and emotions in a journal, you can gain a deeper understanding of who you are and what causes you to feel bad.

Learning to take a step back from your daily life and reflect on what you think and feel can allow you to see the different factors that influence your actions. It can help you to realize why certain situations make you feel the way that they do and figure out what others are thinking when they act a certain way around you.

2. Talk It Out

Another way to analyze your life's triggers is to talk things over with someone. Not only will this help you feel like you have someone to relate to and confide in, it will also help you recognize what others are thinking and feeling. Talking with others can also be a useful tool as they may be able to see things from another perspective, one that may be different from your own.

How to Talk It Out

Step 1: Choose someone that you can trust to talk to.

Choose someone that you are comfortable talking with and who will be objective enough to guide you in your analysis of the world around you.

Step 2: Tell them everything that is on your mind

Once you are with someone you were planning on talking to, tell them everything on your mind. Make sure that they know as much detail as possible, as it will help them try to make sense of what is bothering you and what they can do to help you. This is an excellent opportunity to reflect on your past and discover some things about yourself so that you can learn from past experiences. It is also a helpful way to examine past emotions and thoughts, as well as their origins. Talking about past events may help you figure out what may have caused these feelings or thoughts.

Tell them everything on your mind, as doing so demonstrates your trust in them. It also shows them how much trust and respect you have for this person, so they will be more likely to listen to your thoughts and feelings.

Step 3: Let them take their time before responding

Ask them for their thoughts on what was said and find out if there were any counterarguments or rebuttals that you should be aware of. Allow them to take their time to think about what you have said and decide if they agree with it or not.

If they don't agree with your thoughts or feelings, find out why they feel that way by asking them questions about their views, but make sure that you avoid getting defensive.

Step 4: Let them know what you think and feel.

After you have heard what they have said to you, it is a good idea to let them know what your thoughts and feelings are. Let them know if they have made sense of your situation or if they still don't understand how you feel. If they still don't understand, tell them. You should also try to forgive the person that hurt you in the past, as it will help you move forward.

Step 5: Accept what happened and move on.

Let your conversation with them end and move on. It is also a good idea to share these discussions with others to help you better understand yourself, if possible.

Talking about your past and current experiences will help you understand what has happened in your life and why you feel the way you do. It can help you figure out why someone behaves the way they do, as well as what to do to make sure that things work out well for you. This can also be a good way to figure out what needs to change, as well as how you should deal with things in your life. You can learn what could have been done differently in the past and how to prevent repeating the same mistakes by speaking with others.

3. Consult a Therapist

If you find that talking to others about your triggers is not working for you, it may be time for you to see a therapist. A therapist can help you analyze what is causing your fearful avoidance and help you deal with it differently.

You can learn how to handle this feeling with the help of a good therapist. A therapist will also be able to show you how to control your feelings so that your current situation does not affect your future.

Things to Consider When Choosing a Therapist

Before choosing a therapist, you should consider the following:

a. The Experience of the Therapist.

You must choose a therapist who is knowledgeable about your specific set of problems. Before choosing a therapist, ask them about their past experiences and see if they have worked with people like you. You should also talk to current clients and see what they think about their therapist and how long they have been working with this person. Make sure that you are seeing someone who specializes in your specific situation and age group.

b. How Many Sessions Does the Therapist Offer?

Make sure that you know how many sessions are offered by the therapist. You should make sure that you know when and if the therapist's schedule will allow you to see them again. Not all therapists offer unlimited sessions, so make sure you know exactly how long it will take for them to help you with your situation.

c. Will the Therapist See You regularly?

Make sure you are aware of how frequently you will see the therapist. If you are not seeing them often, it could take longer for them to deal with your situation and help you figure out why you are feeling the way you do. A good therapist can schedule regular interviews with their clients so they can monitor their situations and deal with them quickly and efficiently.

d. Is the Therapist Easy to Work With?

Also consider how easy the therapist is to work with. If you work with a therapist who makes you feel powerless and incapable of making changes in your life, it will be harder for you to deal with your situation. A good therapist can guide you through your issues in a way that is easy for you to understand.

Speak with your therapist and tell them exactly how you are feeling. This is important because they will be able to tell you what has caused your fears and how to deal with your situation. They can also help you figure out what to change to ensure that these situations do not happen again.

Knowing your triggers is not just about understanding your feelings; it is also important to understand how others in your life can trigger them. It is important to understand the effect that someone's actions can have on you, especially if they cause you to become fearful of certain things. Understanding your triggers and the best way to prevent them in the future is crucial.

CHAPTER 8

MANAGING YOUR EMOTIONS

Emotions are powerful, and they can either overpower you or help you. Learning how to manage your emotions and keep them under control is an important part of overcoming your fearful avoidance attachment.

It is important to understand that some emotions are not possible to avoid, but they can be managed in a way that will not harm or affect you. It is also important to learn the difference between an emotion you can do something about and irrational emotion that should not be dealt with. It can sometimes make things easier to stay in control of your emotions if you know exactly what type of emotional response you are going to have or what type of emotional responses you may be trying to avoid.

Learning how to deal with your emotional responses will help you ensure that everything works well for you. Emotions are necessary for life, and we must learn how to manage them properly. A therapist or other mental health expert can help you do this.

Techniques to Manage Your Emotions

Many techniques have been proven to help people keep their emotions under control. If you feel your emotions could be getting the best of you, it is often a good idea to try using some of these techniques to ensure you don't become overwhelmed.

1. Cognitive Distraction

Cognitive distraction is a form of distraction that involves creating lots of distracting thoughts or ideas in your mind. This can help you avoid having a strong emotional connection with the situation or person that is causing you to feel uncomfortable.

Cognitive distraction is a fancy way of saying "get your mind off it." When you feel overly emotional about something, it can often be helpful to take your mind off it and focus on something else. It works by helping you realize that the situation is not nearly as critical or dangerous as your emotional response has made it seem. It also helps you focus on something genuinely positive, which usually helps you regain some perspective.

There are numerous methods for doing this; pick the one that works best for you.

a. Exercise

Exercise releases endorphins and other chemicals that help you to feel good and happy. The effect of exercise on your body and mind is very rewarding, and can provide a healthy distraction from unpleasant emotions and stress.

Some Exercise Ideas:

1. Go for a walk in the park.

Walking is among the most effective and convenient forms of exercise. It is a great way to distract yourself from your problems and have fun. Walking is also very cheap, easy, and accessible, which makes it a great choice if you are short on time or have limited access to exercise equipment. This is also a good choice if you are trying to avoid overdoing it and overexerting yourself.

Walking for at least 15 to 30 minutes each day is recommended. This will give you a good cardiovascular workout and help you to feel healthy, happy, and relaxed afterward. It can be beneficial to walk at different times throughout the day. You are free to choose whenever is most convenient for you, but it is often best to schedule outdoor walks during the day when there are many other people around. This will provide more social stimulation and help you have more positive interactions, in addition to giving your body the exercise it needs.

2. Go for a bike ride.

Biking is another great exercise idea that requires no special equipment or training. It is also accessible and affordable, as most people have bikes at home. Biking is a good choice if you want to get lots of exercise, but you don't want to be too far from your home.

Another advantage of biking is that it doesn't require much in the way of transportation or commuting time. You can ride your bicycle almost anywhere without having to worry about traffic or how long it will take to reach your destination. If you want to get a lot of physical activity without leaving the comfort and safety of your neighborhood or home, cycling is a good option.

3. Go for a run.

This is another form of exercise that doesn't require any special equipment or training. It is also very cheap, accessible, and requires little time and energy to start. Running is a good choice if you want to get a lot of exercise quickly, as it can challenge you physically and help your body get fit more quickly than walking or biking. The only downside of running is that it can make you feel tired afterward, which means that you may need to give yourself some time to recover before doing anything else. Alternatively, you may want to limit your running routine so you don't overdo it too often.

4. Use an exercise DVD.

Many different exercise DVDs can be found at the mall, your local library, or online. Each one will have a different focus, so it is important to choose an exercise routine that will give you the workout that you want and need.

Another option is to search for fitness videos on Youtube and other social media. Since fitness videos are much more easily accessible on social media than they are in most stores and libraries, it will be much simpler for you to find something that meets your needs and preferences. Youtube also has many different types of videos, so it should be easy to find something that matches your personal needs and preferences.

Checking out online exercise videos is also a great way to get motivated and inspired by someone who is achieving the same goals as you. This can help you to feel like you aren't alone and encourages you to keep up with your fitness routine.

5. Do some gardening.

Gardening can be a very enjoyable form of exercise that helps you to get some fresh air while improving your home environment at the same time. This is also a good choice if you like to spend time outdoors and want to do something that will help you and your family to feel healthy, happy, and relaxed.

Gardening is also a good source of physical exercise. For those who are short on time, money, or other resources, it is a fantastic option because it is a cheap exercise that doesn't call for any specialized gear or training.

If you don't have a backyard or a balcony, you can choose to go outside and take part in a community gardening project. You may be able to find one of these at your local church, community center, or other public place. This can give you more social stimulation and help you to feel more involved with your community at the same time.

Exercise is a good habit to form if you want to feel relaxed, happy, and healthy. Any of the many exercise options can be worked into your daily schedule. Be careful, however, not to use them as a crutch or an excuse for ignoring your problems.

b. Meditation

You can unwind, concentrate, and feel more in control of your thoughts and emotions by engaging in meditation, which is an extremely effective type of cognitive distraction. As a result, you will be more productive at work or school and experience fewer stresses from daily life. It is a great way to sharpen your focus and cultivate mindfulness.

Meditation is not quite as convenient as other forms of cognitive distraction because it requires time, energy, and effort to learn how to do it properly. However, the benefits you will get from it are well worth the small effort involved in learning to meditate.

How to do it:

Step 1: Look for a peaceful area to sit.

Find a quiet place where you can meditate without being interrupted or distracted by your surroundings. This may only require you to sit at a desk in your home or place of business, or may require you to travel to another location, such as the library, your backyard, or a park. Choose somewhere that feels comfortable and has a soothing atmosphere so that you will feel relaxed.

Step 2: Find a comfortable position.

Sit up straight in a position that makes you feel relaxed and supported but still gives your body the freedom to move around and breathe comfortably. You can sit in a chair, on the floor, cross-legged, or any other way that makes you feel comfortable.

Step 3: Set an alarm.

Set this up in advance so you don't have to stop in the middle of your meditation to find your phone or clock.

Step 4: Prepare yourself.

Get into the right mindset before starting to meditate. It may be helpful to prepare yourself by appreciating something you have in your life. This can be something simple like appreciating the air you breathe to something as complicated as thanking God or the universe for being alive and for giving you another day on this planet. Find something that will help you focus your thoughts and bring a sense of positivity and gratitude into your life.

Step 5: Breathe.

Now that you have found yourself in the right mindset and have prepared yourself mentally, it is time to focus on your breathing. Take in air through your nose and exhale it through your mouth. You can also close your eyes to help you concentrate on the area of your body used to breathe. Try to stay calm, no matter how difficult or painful it may be.

Step 6: Start focused breathing.

This is it! Now you are ready to start concentrating on the aspect of meditation that you want most out of this exercise – deep concentration and calm, focused breathing. Focus on each breath for two or three seconds before moving on to the next.

Step 7: Return to your breath.

If you find yourself losing concentration, redirect your attention back to your breathing. The more concentrated and focused you are during this exercise, the deeper and more relaxed your mind will become, which is what meditation is all about in the first place.

You will feel more at ease, focused, and in deeper control of your thoughts and emotions after completing these seven steps. This relaxation will help you feel happier and more content with yourself and your life. You should also feel rejuvenated in general and have improved focus on important things like work, school, or other daily activities that are causing you stress. It is therefore an effective tool for dealing with problems or stressful situations that arise throughout your day.

c. Music

You can unwind, concentrate, and feel more in control of your thoughts and emotions by listening to music, which is another excellent method of cognitive diversion. In addition, it is a good way to improve your concentration and mindfulness, which will make you more productive at work or school and alleviate some of the stress of daily life at home.

Music is widely available worldwide. Different music is available for everyone's preferences. Multiple benefits come along with listening to music, including reduced stress levels, improved memory, enhanced creativity, less boredom, better sleep problems and reduced anxiety and depression.

Some may argue that you can find a more effective and efficient way to relax than listening to music. However, this is merely a matter of opinion. If you enjoy listening to music in the privacy and comfort of your own home or place of employment, do so.

d. Prayer

If you are religious, praying can be a great way to distract you from all the thoughts, stress, and troubles that weigh you down throughout your day. This can also be a great way to feel more relaxed, focused, and in control of your emotions since you will be asking for help from someone who is much more powerful than you. Consider this meditation technique with as much openness as you can, and don't judge it or yourself for using it—essentially, it's a way for you to learn how to make changes in your life that work best for you.

e. Breathing Exercises

Breathing exercises are similar to meditating in that they are methods used to improve health, calm the mind, and focus more on their physical and mental wellbeing. It is best to practice breathing exercises when you are not busy but need a distraction.

Some Breathing Exercises:

1. 4-7-8 Counting Breathing

The most common one is the 4-7-8 breathing exercise, also called the "relaxing breath."

How to do it:

Step 1: Breathe in for 4 seconds

Take a deep breath of air (as deeply as feels comfortable and natural to you) through your mouth to the count of 4.

Step 2: Seven seconds of breath holding

Hold the air you have just taken in to the count of seven, or as long as you are comfortable, and then keep it there.

Step 3: Breathe out for 8 seconds

Exhaling the air you have been holding to the count of 8.

This is the ideal breathing pattern you should try to mimic to feel relaxed, focused, and in control of your anxiety and emotions. This is also a good exercise to help you regain control when stress, anxiety, or frustration are getting the best of you throughout your day.

2. Spinal Breathing

Spinal breathing is another common breathing pattern that benefits someone with anxiety or stress. This can be accomplished by focusing on a few specific back muscles, which can help alleviate some of the tension you experience when dealing with stressors and problems in your life.

How to do it:

Step 1: Stand up straight and inhale through your nose as deeply as you can without making it uncomfortable for yourself. Do this until you feel that your lungs are full of air.

Step 2: As long as it feels comfortable, hold the breath you just took.

Step 3: Exhale deeply until you feel all the air is leaving your lungs.

Step 4: Repeat.

This exercise is a great way to release some tension when you are feeling tense or anxious. Additionally, it can be used to enhance your creativity and focus, both of which can improve your performance at work or school.

3. Knee-to-knee breathing

Knee-to-knee breathing is a technique that can help with your concentration, but it can also help you relax and focus more on yourself.

How to do it:

You can perform this easy exercise in any position you like, but lying down is the most efficient.

Step 1: Inhale as deeply as possible through your nose and into your lungs to the count of 8.

Step 2: Exhale for the same number of seconds you inhaled.

Step 3: Breathe normally and relax until you feel ready to repeat the exercise.

When you want to get more out of your concentration, focus more on your breathing, or be more relaxed throughout the day, it would be beneficial to follow these steps. It can also be used when you are trying to control your emotions or feelings.

Learning how to breathe correctly positively impacts your health and wellbeing.

Cognitive distractions are a good way to deal with the stresses and problems you have in your everyday life. It helps manage the emotions of someone with fearful avoidant attachment by calming the mind down. Cognitive distraction benefits anyone who uses it, but it is not a permanent solution to your problems. The trick is to use it as much as possible, so you begin to focus on the positive more than the negative. If you are trying to overcome something, then there will always be a challenge, but over time, you will learn how to solve some of these problems and have more positive days ahead of you.

2. Cognitive Reframing

Cognitive reframing is a technique where you change how you think about whatever you are dealing with. It helps someone realize that things aren't always as bad as they appear, which can make a significant difference in how they deal with stress and other issues.

It is helpful with managing emotions for someone with fearful avoidant attachment because it helps them take control of their anxiety and frustration. By altering your perspective on particular matters, you can make coping with them easier.

The following are a few different methods that can be used to create cognitive reframing:

a. Positive Affirmations

Words have the power to move people, and they can also cause someone to feel negative emotions, or like they want to improve themselves. Positive affirmations are a great way to alter your perspective on a situation. They work by saying out loud or in the head things that you want to be true about something so you can make it a reality. This can help you feel better about yourself, and it makes it easier for you to deal with your problems.

Some Positive Affirmations:

"I am loved now, and this is going to be the best thing that has ever happened to me."

"I am going to fix my problem and make it better, so I feel great."

"My friends and family love me no matter what I do, so I should be perfectly fine telling them how I feel."

"Next time things are difficult for me, I'll try to remember that these things won't last forever. The people who care about me always help me through these times of trouble."

"I can do anything I want to, so don't let anyone tell me I can't."

"This is going to be the best day of my life, and I am going to feel great."

"I am happy now and want to make sure it stays that way for a long time."

"This feeling is going to go away. I need to get through it, and then I will be fine."

"Because I am a great person, I can do anything I want."

"I know this will be the best day of my life."

"This situation will end soon, and things will be better than ever before!"

"I have so many things going right for me right now that this feeling in the pit of my stomach won't last forever!"

"Everything will turn out for the best!"

"I will do whatever it takes to get through this problem and prove everyone wrong."

"I am a great person, and I always will be, even if this situation doesn't go my way."

"Things are not as bad as they seem; I just need to take a step back and realize that I can do better than this!"

"I will do what it takes to make myself happy!"

b. Visualization

Visualization involves of making a picture in your head of what you want to happen. It can help someone deal with whatever they are going through. This can help someone with fearful avoidant attachment realize that they are better off than they think.

How to do it:

Step 1: Think about the situation you are in or something you want to change.

This can be big or small, but think about how you want it to look, as if it were finished. Consider what you desire for yourself and how you can achieve it.

Step 2: Make the picture in your head as real as possible.

Make that picture in your head as real as possible, meaning that you spend time making it detailed and real. Think of the colors and where they are positioned in the image; who else is there with you?

Step 3: Let go and accept whatever happens.

When you have finished creating the picture in your head, don't try to control or change anything because the situation will be different from the one you had pictured. Accept this and let yourself feel better about whatever is going on.

Visualization is a great method for those who have forgotten what it feels like to be happy. It helps them focus on the future and their goals.

3. Other Emotion Regulation Strategies

Other types of emotion regulation strategies can also help someone with fearful avoidant attachment. These include:

a. The Squeeze Technique

The Squeeze Technique is a method that uses a squeeze ball or a stress ball to help one relax their muscles. This can help a someone with fearful avoidant attachment ease up on the anxiety they are feeling.

It is suggested that fearful avoidants try this method if they can't seem to get rid of their anxiety even after using cognitive reframing. The squeeze technique is easy, and it doesn't take much time to learn.

How to do it:

Step 1: Hold your stress ball and squeeze it.

Take your stress ball in one hand and squeeze it as hard as possible for about 30 seconds to one minute. Try to squeeze the ball with all the muscles in your hand and arm, including your fingers and knuckles. Squeezing this ball should help you to get rid of some of the tension in your body.

Step 2: Release the tension on the stress ball.

Now, release all of the tension out of your body by letting go of the stress ball. Notice how much better that feels than having a fist full of sharp knuckles. Remember what it feels like not to have so much tension in your body and pay attention to how that feels.

Step 3: Practice a few times a day.

Practice this method whenever you feel anxious or are dealing with any difficult situation. It doesn't take long for you to get used to this method, and it is always easy to use. If you try it a few times, you will probably see results in how you feel after doing the exercise. It is also fairly cheap, so if you do need another stress ball for one reason or another, it shouldn't be too expensive to get one.

b. Progressive Muscle Relaxation Technique

This is a relaxational method that helps a someone to focus on all the different muscles in the body and determine which muscle groups need to be relaxed. This method can help those with fearful avoidant attachment relax their muscles when they become tense or stressed out.

How to do it:

Step 1: Find a comfortable spot and focus on your breathing.

Find a comfortable spot to sit down and focus on your breathing. Observe the air that enters and leaves your body as you breathe. Try not to think about anything else except your breathing. Try to let go of all thoughts about your day and focus only on the tension leaving and entering your body as you breathe.

Step 2: Focus on each muscle group you will be working on.

Now, focus on one muscle group by moving the muscles in that area. Start by focusing on your toes, then your calves, then your thighs, then your chest, abs, and shoulders. Concentrate on each part of your body separately to help you become more relaxed.

You will feel a warm sensation in your body when you focus on a specific muscle group. That is because your muscles will start to get warm as you are focusing on them and as you are relaxing them. This muscle relaxation method is great for those with fearful avoidant attachment. It helps to relax the muscles and makes it easier to focus on the problem rather than worrying about your anxiety or stress levels.

Step 3: When you are done, relax your body and focus on breathing.

Once you have focused on each muscle group, then you will feel more relaxed overall. Once this happens, relax your body by making it as limp as possible while also focusing on breathing. It is important to be able to breathe freely when you are trying to get rid of tension in the body.

The best time for doing this method is either before going to sleep at night or when you wake up so the muscles are completely relaxed.

c. The 15-minute Rule

The 15-minute rule is a little different than the previous relaxation techniques. It involves focusing on what you are feeling right now because fearful avoidants might be overloaded with information or worrying about something that has happened in the past and how it will affect them in the future. This method helps to let go of all of that excess information and worrying by moving forward in time.

How to do it:

Step 1: Focus on what you want to get rid of.

Start by concentrating on what you wish to eliminate, whether that involves letting go of something from your past or something that is bothering you in the present. Whatever it is, focus on that thought so that you can let go of it and move beyond or away from whatever it is. This method will help clear your mind so that you can become less worried and distracted. The 15-minute rule focuses on the future and moving forward instead of the past.

Step 2: Focus inwardly on yourself.

Now, focus inwardly on yourself. Think about anything or everything bothering you and then let go of it. The key to this method is to move through the thoughts and worry immediately because if you keep moving forward through them, they will disappear over time. Do this for 15 minutes.

Step 3: Relax your body and focus on breathing.

When 15 minutes is up, relax your body and then focus on your breathing by making it deep as possible. This kind of relaxation is helpful because it allows you to become more relaxed than before. The more relaxed someone becomes, the less anxious they will feel overall.

If the bothersome thought persists after focusing on your breathing, proceed with the fifteen-minute rule again.

d. The Unforgivable Acts Technique

This is a simple but effective way to get rid of whatever is bothering you. This method will allow you to focus on what has happened and let it go because you won't be thinking about it anymore after practicing this method.

How to do it:

Step 1: Think about what you want to forget.

The initial step is to determine what you wish to forget. It could be an image, a thought, or just a feeling. You can also focus on both someone else's actions and your reaction towards that thing. Think back on whatever happened in as much detail as possible. If it is something that someone else has done to you, then imagine what happened from their point of view and think about how you would react if you were them.

This step is crucial because it enables fearful avoidants to let go of their problems through in-depth reflection. Thinking about a situation in great detail will allow them to understand why they feel the way they do and why they are thinking about a particular problem or thought. After focusing on why someone feels the way they do and where their thoughts are coming from, they can focus on forgetting everything by letting go of it completely.

Step 2: Let go.

After you have gone over what happened in great detail in your head, allow yourself to completely forget about the specific problem. It shouldn't take more than two to three minutes to forget everything.

Step 3: Relax

If you can completely let go after you have done this technique, relax by doing some deep breathing. This kind of relaxation allows you to focus on staying positive for the rest of your life.

Managing your emotions and avoiding unnecessary negative thoughts can be difficult, but it is something that you can learn how to do over time. You can start to overcome your past by making the right decisions in your life, and using the right management techniques. If you want to live a better life, then these management techniques is a great way to do so.

CHAPTER 9

BOOSTING MY SELF ESTEEM

Self-esteem is an important trait to develop. It is related to our self-image and how we perceive what we are. Fearful avoidants usually have low self-esteem. This is because their self-image is based on their self-doubt and their fears of being treated or shunned.

Advantages of Having High Self-esteem

1. Better Relationships

Lower self-esteem can make you feel inferior, shy, and withdrawn. It is hard to make friends and become part of a group if you constantly feel like an outsider.

Self-confidence is the key to becoming a more approachable person and enjoying better connections with others. Someone with low self-esteem often cannot communicate well in relationships because they doubt their worth as a human and don't feel that they deserve positive attention.

As a fearful avoidant, you need to learn to connect with others. Having high self-esteem will help you do this since it makes you more confident. Forming relationships and communicating with others will allow you to find and maintain a good balance in your life without as much anxiety as before.

2. Less Stress

Someone with low self-esteem may feel stressed out and overwhelmed most of the time. They frequently feel as though they do not have enough time to complete all of their responsibilities or devote enough time to their hobbies and interests because they believe so much else must be completed. Those with high self-esteem, on the other hand, have a deeper sense of peace and a lower level of stress in their daily lives.

This confidence may also protect a someone from anxiety-related situations such as fear of failure or social anxiety. It allows someone to trust in themselves and know that they won't fail or do something embarrassing. As a result, the stress response will not be activated, and the anxiety experienced won't be as high.

This feeling of peace and confidence may also allow them to see someone more positively and form relationships with strangers who are kind-hearted instead of cold-hearted. This may provide some protection from feelings of insecurity in social situations, which leads to lower stress levels.

As a result of less stress, the body produces more endorphins – the chemicals that boost feelings of wellbeing and relaxation. Higher self-esteem also means you're more likely to eat healthily, exercise more often, and sleep well. Your positive energy and confidence can also positively affect those you're close to, helping to make them feel happier and more relaxed.

3. Less Anxiety & Depression

As you develop more confidence and self-esteem, you'll be able to think of yourself as someone who is not easily affected by negativity and harsh criticism from others. Those with low self-esteem will usually become anxious at the smallest of issues. Still, as you become more resilient to stress, this anxiety will reduce and eventually leave altogether.

It's also believed that self-confidence can reduce or even help prevent symptoms of depression and anxiety since it improves your ability to cope with everyday life. Someone with low self-esteem may experience anxiety in unusual situations such as having their partner leave them or being unable to cope with home responsibilities.

4. More Successful

Great self-confidence allows you to see the opportunities and rewards that are present before you, thus making you more successful in work or other areas of life. You will be more likely to believe that miracles happen when things look impossible, which could help you find a new job or opportunity. This self-confidence may also lead you to pursue your hobbies and personal interests more successfully, giving you a very positive outlook on life.

Someone is more likely to exert effort if they have a higher degree of self-assurance. Confidence allows someone to do more of what they're good at, which helps them achieve greater success. This, in turn, will increase their confidence even further.

5. More Support & Encouragement

If you have low self-esteem, you may believe you don't have enough support and encouragement from others in times of need, which may make it difficult to gain the motivation to continue fighting through a tough situation. Meanwhile, those with high self-esteem feel more confident that they have some-one there to support them when they need it. This could be friends, family, or even a professional who offers advice and medical care.

When you are confident, you'll attract more people who are pleased with your success and want to support and encourage you further. This can give you a stronger drive to succeed and continue contributing to society.

6. More Creative

Someone with low self-esteem is often less interested in things considered "creative" or challenging. Research has found that, as you become more confident in yourself, you will be more likely to think positively and have a greater understanding of how to see challenges as opportunities. You have learned how to overcome the obstacles in life, and your creativity will increase greatly. As a result, you'll be able to see new possibilities and ways of interacting with the world around you. You'll also begin making new connections with people who share similar interests and values.

This broader perspective of life will also allow you to think of new possibilities that may not have been apparent to you before. This can be the difference between a person struggling to find work and someone who has made a successful career. As your confidence continues to grow, so will your creativity, which will make you even more successful in whatever you do.

Even in stressful or difficult circumstances, research has shown that positive thinking can boost creativity and increase productivity. This confidence can help you move forward despite setbacks or challenging circumstances and make better decisions, rather than giving up too soon or making poor choices because of stress and anxiety.

7. More Happiness

Those with low self-esteem usually feel like they aren't living the life they want. This may lead to depression and anxiety, which can be difficult to overcome. However, someone with high self-esteem generally feels happier with themselves and content in their everyday life.

While this will not solve all of your problems overnight, it is a healthier state of mind that will help you live a more fulfilling and satisfying life. You won't need to constantly compare yourself to others or spend so much energy on negative thoughts about yourself. Instead, you'll have more confidence, making you happy and content with the life you currently have.

If you just had a little extra self-confidence, it could mean the difference between a lifetime of happiness and a lifetime of depression.

Ways to Improve Self-Esteem

So what are some ways to increase self-confidence? There are a lot of ways to do this; the following are just a few:

1. Change Your Belief About Yourself

If your self-confidence is not up to par and you need more than just a boost, it's time to change the way that you think about yourself. The following are some ways to do so:

a. Look for the Positives

One way to change your belief is to look for the positive in others and yourself. This will help you see the good things about yourself and others that you may not have noticed before.

This works because it changes your expectations of yourself and others. If you learn to see the good qualities of others and yourself, you will start to conclude that you are also worthy.

How to do this:

Step 1: Pick someone that you think is positive.

This should be someone you respect, someone with a lot of self-confidence, or even your mentor or colleague.

Step 2: Write their positive qualities down.

Write down a list of 3 to 4 positive qualities that you think they have. This list can be about their personality, skills, and/or about how they deal with life. Instead of focusing on their flaws, highlight their strengths.

Step 3: Read over the list; why do you like these things?

After you write the list, read it over again and see if you can identify why you like these qualities about them. Maybe it's because they make someone around them feel important or because they can solve problems effectively, or maybe it's just because they know what they want from life and can follow through with that.

Step 4: Try to incorporate the things you like.

After you have an answer, it's time to take action. You have been able to identify something that makes them a good person, and now it's time for you to incorporate that into your own life. This can be difficult because many people fear change, but remember, not everything has to happen overnight. If something doesn't work for you, then don't force it. Try something else until you find something that works for you.

b. The SCRIP Technique

This was developed by Albert Meyers, founder of the Psychotherapy Center in Lake Forest Park, WA. The SCRIP(Self-Confidence In Positive) Technique helps you become more confident by learning how to overcome the negative effects of your past. This can help change the way that you think and feel about yourself.

This strategy is predicated on the notion that everyone has one or two irrational beliefs that affect their regular emotions and behaviors. These beliefs stem from events that happened at an early age, such as your parents arguing when you were younger or someone teasing you for being overweight. They can also be caused by events later in life, such as a bad breakup, someone who said something negative about you behind your back, or if you lost your job.

The SCRIP technique can help you understand the irrational beliefs that may be holding you back from feeling more confident. It helps you learn how to overcome these irrational beliefs and develop rational ones that will contribute to your self-confidence.

How to do it:

Step 1: Identify any irrational beliefs you may have regarding your past experiences.

You may believe that because your parents were arguing or your significant other broke up with you, you are "not good enough," that "nobody likes you," or something else negative.

Identifying these irrational beliefs can be difficult, and you may need to ask for help from friends or family members. This is a crucial step, as skipping it will prevent you from overcoming your irrational beliefs and will instead cause you to continue feeling self-conscious.

Step 2: Find evidence that contradicts the irrational belief.

This is the step where you will learn how to overcome the negative feelings that stem from whatever event or situation happened in your past. Think back and try to remember a time when you felt good about yourself despite whatever happened in your past.

Step 3: Try to feel the positive emotion you felt during the event.

By focusing on this positive emotion, you will feel more self-assured and proud of who you are. This is the part that is difficult for most people because it requires you to remember and experience a positive feeling from something in your past. If it's too hard to do on your own, ask a friend or a family member for help. They may be able to trigger the feeling in your memory and make it easier for you.

By feeling more positive, you can eliminate the irrational belief that has been holding you back.

Step 4: Replace the old belief with a new rational one.

When you feel confident and proud of yourself, it will be easier to replace the old irrational belief with a new rational one. This is just reinforcing your confidence and pride in who you are. By doing this, you will have a more positive outlook on yourself and will be less likely to feel negatively in your future.

Step 5: Find ways to practice your new rational belief.

This can help you overcome the negative thinking that may have been holding you back up to this point. Practicing these new beliefs will help reinforce your self-confidence.

As you continue to work on this, you may begin to feel even stronger feelings about yourself because of all of the things that have been done so far. The process will take some time, but it will all be worthwhile if you persevere.

c. Stop Comparing Yourself to Others

You'll start to feel insecure and unworthy if you keep comparing yourself to others. Just focus on how you feel about yourself.

Your self-confidence is determined by how you feel about yourself, and it makes no difference what anyone else thinks of you. It's crucial to avoid comparing yourself to others because this will make you insecure.

Just because someone can do better than you at something, it does not mean that there's something wrong with you or that they are better than you. It's important to remember that we are all unique and have different skills. Instead of comparing your actual aptitude or skills to those of others, try comparing your growth. You will be able to feel more confident and will be less likely to think negatively about yourself.

2. Develop Positive Motivators and Habits

Developing new positive habits and developing your motivation is crucial to boosting your self-esteem. This will lead you to feel better about yourself and your life in general and will help you take control of your success. Just like the saying, "If you fail to plan, then you plan to fail," you will also fail if you don't have the right motivation and habits to get things done.

Learning how to develop positive motivators and habits can help you feel better about yourself. Some of these habits may seem hard to do at first, but they are worth it in the long run.

When you start by focusing on your positive motivators, then follow through with them by developing habits, you are putting yourself partially back in control of your own life. This can be very helpful for those who typically lack the motivation to finish tasks on their own or who just need a little push in the right direction.

The following is a list of positive motivators that you can focus on to begin improving your self-esteem:

a. Love Yourself

It's extremely difficult to do this step because it requires you to start looking at yourself differently. You must make a conscious effort to focus on all the positive aspects of yourself rather than all the flaws you see in yourself. This will get simpler over time.

You can do a lot of things to improve your ability for self-love, including:

1. Spending time with your family and friends

Spending time with others can be very beneficial. Showing appreciation for others in your life is a very good way to build your self-esteem.

2. Getting in shape

As you begin to work out, you will learn many great things about yourself that you may not have known before. This will build your self-confidence, and self-esteem will start to grow.

3. Be Social

If life is hard for you, then make an effort to spend time with someone who can help you improve things for the better. Being social is a great way to build your self-esteem, and you'll love yourself for it.

4. Do good work

This will also help boost your self-confidence and self-esteem because you will be doing something important and meaningful to others, making you proud of yourself.

5. Be yourself

Being yourself is what matters, not what someone thinks of you. This is a very important concept because it can boost your self-esteem greatly if you learn how to accept things the way that they are instead of trying to change them.

6. Look at the bright side of things

This can help you get better at turning bad situations into positive ones and accept the negatives in life. This will have a great impact on self-esteem and confidence as well.

7. Be honest with yourself

Being honest with yourself can boost your self-esteem and confidence to new levels.

8. Making new friends

This is an important one. Having new friends can make a huge difference in your life because it will help you feel better about yourself.

9. Learn to say no

A lot of people struggle with this very important concept because they don't want to hurt others or let anyone down. However, learning to say no can boost your self-esteem because you will learn how to protect yourself from bad situations and relationships.

How to say no:

- It's all about understanding how you feel and what you want.

- Don't try to set rules because it will make it easier for others to manipulate you and steer your feelings.

- If others want something from you that you are unable or unwilling to give, then tell them no. If they don't like that answer, explain that if they don't do what you want them to do, then there will be no more contact with them. If they don't like that idea, then there's your answer.

- It's all about focusing on you, learning how to say no, and making it easier for others to give up on whatever it is that they are asking of you.

b. Do the things you love

When you start to do the things you love, you will feel better about yourself and your life. It's also a great way to start thinking positively, and keep your self-esteem on an even keel.

1. Find a new hobby

If you don't already have one, then it's time to develop new hobbies and interests. This will help you feel better about yourself and the things you have going on in life.

2. Take your time

This is a concept that is very important because it will have a huge impact on everything else that you are trying to do in life. If you take your time and learn how to be patient, it will help you relax and get better at controlling your emotions. Taking your time is also a very important concept. It can help boost self-esteem because it will make you proud of yourself.

3. Don't make excuses

Learning not to make excuses is an important part of building self-esteem and is a great way to move forward in life. This is a very important part of self-improvement.

4. Accept mistakes

You must learn to accept this concept because when we are accepting of our mistakes, they become less painful and easier for us to deal with.

5. Learn to listen

Learning how to listen is a concept that many people struggle with. Still, it's very important in life because it allows you to absorb information and make the best decisions possible.

6. Don't confuse self-confidence with arrogance

You don't have to act differently just because you feel good about yourself. Just because you are developing self-confidence does not mean you should be arrogant about it. Humility is the key.

8. Make an effort to feel good about yourself.

Your self-esteem will increase when you take deliberate actions that make you feel good about yourself. Doing so will help you maintain focus on your priorities. This will not only help you stay on track for the things you desire in life, but it will also help you keep your attention on what is most important to you.

3. Reach Towards Your Goals

Setting goals is one of the best ways to build self-esteem. Achieving your goals will help change your life and make you feel better. It is something you can work on daily.

This will help build positive habits in your life and positive results to go along with them. If you don't know where you're going or when you're going to get there, goals will help give your life direction, which is something everyone needs.

Goals are like a roadmap for the future that give purpose to your life.

The following are ways to move towards your goals:

a. Have a Vision of Excellence

The most important thing to do when it comes to your goals is to have a vision of excellence. This is something that no one can give you; it has to come from within. When you have this vision inside of you, and you have the desire to achieve it, that is enough to get things started.

How to create a vision of excellence:

Step 1: Write down your description of what excellence looks like.

This is your definition of excellence and what it means to be successful. Remember that this may change over time. This can be about your goals, work, home life, or anything else you want to excel in.

This description of your vision should be brief but clear. Make it something that will stick in your mind easily so you can hold onto it and keep referring to it throughout your day.

For example, you may write "I want to be ____________________" (This is your own definition of excellence).

Step 2: Use this vision to help you implement the process.

Refer to this vision when making decisions in your life. For example, when you are trying to decide about something like work, school, or family life, consider how each option will benefit you and make your life better. When this vision is always in use, it will guide everything that happens in your life and keep you on track for the things that matter most to you.

As time goes on, you will develop your own values and style. You will learn this through your experiences and the people you meet.

b. Start at the Beginning

Making sure that you start at the beginning will make things easier.

The beginning is important because it represents your original intention. Think about the goal you want to achieve and where it will lead.

Ask yourself these questions:

- What is the purpose of this goal?

- Where do I want to go with my life?

- What will be my final reward for completing the goal?

Write your answers down in a journal or plan of action so they are available when you need them. This may seem like an extra step, but it's very important because it shows that you have intention with what you want to do in life and where you want to go.

c. Prioritize Your Goals

This is something that most people do not do. Having a good sense of priorities lets you focus on the things that are most important or valuable for the future.

What happens when you don't prioritize your goals?

If you do not have good priorities, it will be hard for you to focus on the most important things in your life. This may result in you losing sight of what is crucial. As a result, you will always make poor decisions because they are inconsistent with your vision of excellence.

This will also help boost your self-esteem because it allows you to prioritize the things that matter most in your life. When you do this, everything else falls into place and you will achieve more positive results in life.

How to prioritize your goals?

Here are the steps to take when you are trying to prioritize your goals. Think about what it means for the future and how it will benefit you in the long run.

Step 1: Be Consistent

Your goals should be consistent with your vision of excellence, meaning they should be directly related to the things you want to achieve. Make sure that you're concentrating on the tasks that are most meaningful and important for your life.

Step 2: Be Clear

The goals should be clear so you understand how they will benefit you. Think about what each goal means for you, where it is leading, and how it will make your life better. If it isn't clear, ask yourself why this is so and what is missing from the goal that will make it more effective.

When your goals are clear and consistent, it will be easier for you to attain them because you will have a road map you can follow. This makes it easier to remember what the goals mean, making it easier to prioritize them and follow through with them in the long run.

Step 3: Be Specific

Your goals should be specific so you know exactly what you are working towards. This ensures you are not wasting time working on things that are not crucial to your life. For example, if your goal is to go back to college, then think about what this means to you and how it will benefit you over the long term.

When your goals are specific, there is a good chance that they will lead to success in the long run and allow you to reach more positive results in life.

Step 4: Be Timely

To ensure that you are constantly working on something crucial for the future, your goals should be timely.

Example:

"I want to be_____________________ (something significant to you) by_________________ (when?)"

Having a time frame will make it easier for you to focus on the things that are most important, and it will also allow you to set better goals in the long run. Also, when your goals are timely, there is a good chance that you will succeed because you are thinking about the future and what is most important in your life.

Step 5: Keep it Small

It's not good for your goals to be too big for you or to worry about other things that are unrelated to the subject at hand. For example, if you are trying to lose weight, then your goal should be directly tied in with this vision of excellence. If the goal is linked to your vision of excellence, it will be simpler for you to accomplish and progress toward more advantageous outcomes in life.

Your goals will be simple for you to achieve and won't take up much of your time if you keep them modest. This is because it helps you focus on what needs to be done in order to achieve them.

In the end, it's crucial to understand your goals and the directions they are pointing. You should be doing this regularly, and this will help your mind focus on the things that are most important in your life. Having a clear and concise goal will make it easier for you to focus on what matters most to you and your life's direction.

Reaching your goals will lead you towards more positive results in life. It will help you build your self-esteem, make you a better person, and help you do meaningful and important things in your life.

Your self-esteem as a fearful avoidant is important. Having good self-esteem is something that will allow you to be more comfortable in your own skin, help you in your relationships for the future, and also make you a better person inside and out.

Overcoming your fearful avoidant tendencies can be done, and it is important to remember that it is not a one-time thing; you will have to continue working on your mindset, and this will allow you to reach more positive outcomes in life.

You should always be working on improving your self-esteem, getting closer to the vision of excellence that you have for yourself, and also making it easier for you to achieve more positive results in life.

PART 4

LOVING A FEARFUL AVOIDANT PARTNER

CHAPTER 10

PRACTICAL TIPS FOR HELPING A LOVED ONE WITH FEARFUL AVOIDANT TRAITS

Fearful avoidant attachment is the most difficult attachment type to work with, and it can be particularly hard on you if you have a fearful avoidant partner. This chapter provides some advice and suggestions to help you nurture a loving, emotionally supportive relationship with someone with fearful avoidance traits.

Actions You Can Take for a Loved One

1. Practice The 5 A's

The 5 A's are a way to make someone with fearful avoidance traits feel safe and accepted. It's not intended to be a way of "fixing" someone. It's instead a way to help them feel more accepting of themself so that they don't have as much fear or trepidation in relationships. Instead of getting someone with fearful avoidance traits to change and grow, you focus on helping them feel accepted and cared for.

The 5 A's are:

Acceptance

Accept that they are fearful avoidant. They see the world as dangerous and harmful, and they want to spend their lives running away from these dangers. That's how they are. You can't change that, but you can try to accept this about them.

How to do this:

a. Accept that you can't change them

Most of the time, it's best not to try and change someone else. It's important to accept that there are things about your partner, like their personality traits or beliefs, that you must accept. Once we let go of our misguided efforts to control others, we free ourselves to accept and love them for who they are.

b. Set Boundaries

A boundary is one of the most important barriers you can put in place. That sounds harsh, but it's important. Setting and maintaining boundaries will be more difficult if your partner feels unappreciated or rejected. As a result, they'll use manipulation tactics on you – probably subtle ones at first – to keep the relationship going.

c. Acceptance is Healing

Fearful avoidants often feel rejected, so low self-esteem and frustration usually set in. This makes it challenging for them to feel truly alive and joyful, as you can probably imagine. Even if you disagree with all of their beliefs or decisions, if you can accept them for who they are, they will start to feel more comfortable in their own skin. They'll feel less rejection and, consequently, less fear and resentment.

Accepting someone for who they are – even if you don't agree with everything they do – is an important step toward helping them become more open, caring, and loving.

Appreciation

Appreciation is a way to show your partner that you love them for who they are. It's not a way to get something in return, but rather that you notice their good traits and love them for it.

How to do this:

a. Take notice of their good qualities

One of the most common mistakes someone with fearful avoidant traits makes is putting up walls or withdrawing when something or someone is good for them. They can find it hard to believe that anything or anyone could be good for them, so they reject those things.

You can help your partner by noticing all the things they do well. It will help to reduce the amount of fear and rage that goes on inside of their mind. As a result, you'll feel more connected and closer than ever before.

b. Praise them

Praise your partner for all that they do or say for you (and others) and for the contributions they make to the world as another way of expressing your love and gratitude. By letting them know when they say or do something admirable, you can demonstrate your love for your spouse.

c. Comfort them when necessary

It can also help to comfort your partner when they're hurt, upset, or frightened. Sometimes, it's not enough to acknowledge their pain; you have to comfort them and make them feel better. Being present for someone when they need you most, both physically and emotionally, is frequently the best thing you can do for them. You'll be surprised how much appreciation and gratitude your partner will feel if you do this for them.

d. Appreciate their efforts

One of the things that fearful avoidants attachment do well work hard at what they do. They frequently exert a lot of effort to complete tasks effectively. It's important to let them know that you appreciate their effort, even if they make mistakes or don't succeed at what they set out to do. As far as your partner is concerned, it's not how well something goes that's important – it's how much effort was put into it. Appreciating your partner is a way of showing them that you love them and care about them. This will help to reduce their fear and anxiety.

Action

This is a great way to express your love for someone. And it's not only for romantic partners or married couples. It's a way to show that you care and that you can show your appreciation in many different ways.

How to do this:

a. Listen

One of the things fearful avoidants find challenging is express-ing their gratitude and love to others. As a result, they may shut down when you try to thank them for something or show them how much you care.

You can help your partner feel loved by showing that you want to listen to them. If they want to tell you more about something, tell them that you're ready, listening, and willing. Your partner will feel valued and cared for if they know someone wants to listen to what's going on in their mind – even if it isn't flattering or desirable.

b. Compliment

It can be hard for someone with this type of attachment to feel appreciated. They constantly feel like they're being criticized or judged and that their goodness isn't winning any praise or attention.

You can help them feel more appreciated by complimenting them on how good they are at something. Even if it's not very flattering, tell your partner that you think they're wonderful at what they do. They'll love hearing it and will feel valued for who they are.

c. Free them from their worries

When your partner is fearful and avoidant, one thing that gets on their nerves is being told that they need to change or be fixed in some way. They're afraid that if they change, their partner will see them as less than worthy or valuable. They therefore attempt to conceal their issues, worries, or anxieties from you.

d. Encourage them to take risks

Fear-based thinking is one thing that binds someone with fearful avoidant attachment. They think negatively and can't get out of that negative headspace without your help. So encourage them to take risks with you and trust you all over again; show them that they can trust you and that it's safe for them to be who they are – flaws, insecurities, and all.

e. Lower their defenses

When your partner feels devalued, it's hard for them to lower their defenses. It's almost like they're saying: "You'll only hurt me if I let you in." But you can help them lower their defenses by showing that you understand that they're feeling hurt, rejected, or angry and that you accept that they feel that way.

Taking action shows your partner that you can love them for who they are and that you won't walk away from them. This will help them feel safe and accepted.

Affection

Affection is a great way to show your love for someone. It lets them know that you care about them, and that you want to be close to them.

How to do this:

a. Reassure them that you're not trying to change them

Sometimes, fearful avoidants feel like their partner is trying to criticize them by showing affection. Therefore, it's critical to reassure them that your goal is to express your love and appreciation for who they are as they are rather than to change them. This way, your partner will continue to feel loved for who they are.

b. Remember that affection doesn't have to mean sex

Fearful avoidants worry that their partners will expect sex as a way of showing love. And they worry that when they don't want to do it, their partner will be upset or disappointed in them.

You can help your partner by remembering that affection doesn't always mean sex. You can show your partner how much you care about them by giving them a kiss on the forehead, on the cheek, or holding hands when you're out together.

The key thing is to make your gestures romantic and loving. And remember that you don't need to hold hands or kiss all the time for your affection to have value.

c. Tell them how they make you feel

It's important for fearful avoidants to feel loved and connected in a relationship. If they feel like they're being loved, appreciated, and valued, it'll help them feel safe and secure in the relationship.

Show your partner that they make you feel loved by telling them so.

d. Spend quality time with them

Spending quality time together is important, especially if your partner is prone to fear-based thinking. Defenses are the natural response to being rejected or abandoned. It's important for your partner to feel like they matter and that they're not being tossed aside by their attachment style.

With a fearful avoidant attachment, it can be hard for them to feel valued and loved due to low insecurities and sensitivity. You can make sure they feel loved by spending quality time with them.

e. Show them that you're willing to be vulnerable

Fearful avoidants are afraid of being vulnerable with their partner. This is because they're afraid their partner will reject or abandon them if they show vulnerability.

Giving your partner a gift, taking them out, or telling them how much they mean to you are all effective ways to demonstrate your willingness to show vulnerability. You may feel safer and more attracted to one another as a result.

Aspiration

Whether or not your partner has fearful avoidant attachment, you can make them feel better by showing them your aspirations for the relationship. Let them know that you care about them and want to grow along with them as you create something together.

How to do this:

a. Show them that you want to grow together

Those with fearful avoidant attachment often feel like their partner doesn't care about them, and that they don't matter to their partner. You can show your partner that they make you grow as a person by giving them space when they need it or listening when they have something important to say.

Most fearful avoidants like to be independent and don't want others to intrude on their personal space. They also worry that their partner will hurt or abandon them if they open up. So it's important for them to feel like you want to build something together.

b. Show them that you want to make the relationship work

Fearful avoidants are often insecure in their relationships due to distrust, insecurities, and hypersensitivity. Therefore, it's important for you to reassure them that you want to make things work.

Let your partner know that you could never imagine making it through life without them and reassure them that they make your life better. It would also help if you showed them how much they mean to you by spending time with them and showing your feelings of affection.

You can also show your partner that you want to make things work by being honest with them. If you're feeling something, let them know! It doesn't hurt to be honest about how you feel about certain things so long as it's not hurtful or rude.

c. Be truthful

Be honest about your feelings with your partner. But make sure to do so in a way that shows how much you care about them. If you don't like something they've done, tell them so you can work things out. Show your partner that you care by being open and honest with them about how you feel.

d. Help them find their purpose in life

By making sure your partner is happy every day and assisting them in discovering their purpose in life, you can demonstrate your concern for them. However, they like to be independent and don't want others to intrude on their personal space. They also worry that their partner will hurt or abandon them if they open up. So it's important for them to feel like you want to build something together.

Practicing the 5 A's with your partner helps make you and your partner feel closer and safe in the relationship. The 5 A's will help you show your partner that they matter to you, that they're well-respected and loved, and that they're simply part of a great loving team.

2. Conflict Resolution

Conflicts are inevitable when it comes to relationships, but conflict resolution can make or break a relationship. Being able to resolve conflicts effectively with your partner can show them that they're safe and secure with you.

The following are ways you can use conflict resolution to build trust and security in your relationship:

Step 1: Recognize Unresolved Conflicts

Recognizing a conflict between you and your partner is the first step in solving it amicably. Don't just brush the problem under the rug – address the problem head-on and talk it out with your partner. Communication is very important in relationships, so make sure that you give your partner enough time to express their feelings and concerns.

Recognizing unresolved conflicts is important because it helps you and your partner be open and honest with each other. It encourages a healthy respect for their feelings and needs rather than putting them down or ignoring them.

How to do this:

1. Take turns expressing feelings

When you and your partner are arguing, take turns expressing your feelings. You could even write things down, so you have a record of what was said and why.

Talk about the problem or disagreement while looking into each other's eyes instead of in the distance. Or sit next to each other instead of across from each other while you discuss the problem.

2. Listen to them and validate their feelings

This step is a big step in conflict resolution – you must listen to your partner and validate their feelings. Make sure they understand that they're safe with you.

You can even use humor or fun anecdotes to break the tension. Humor helps diffuse the situation and may make your partner feel more comfortable.

Listen to your partner, assist them in understanding their needs, wants, and problems, and then check to see if everything went well. This will show your partner that you value them.

Recognizing unresolved conflicts will give you and your partner the chance to discuss your problems so you can figure out a solution or at least stop the argument. Recognizing unresolved conflicts is the first step in conflict resolution. You can ensure that you both feel safe and secure by speaking honestly and paying attention to each other.

Step 2: Find a Solution

The next step in conflict resolution is finding a solution to the problem, so everyone involved is happy.

Finding a solution is important because it helps makes sure your partner feels safe and secure with you. It can also keep both of you from arguing. The last thing you want to do after resolving conflicts with your partner is fight about another issue.

How to do this:

1. Think through solutions together

Make sure you give your partner enough time to think about a solution and work together to come up with something that makes everyone happy. If possible, bring up different solutions together so your partner feels like their opinion matters.

This will demonstrate your concern for them and your respect for their viewpoints. You'll have to be patient, but it will make a difference in the long run.

2. Reach an agreement

After you and your partner think of a solution, reach an agreement together. You'll want to find an agreement that makes everyone happy – don't just decide for both of you. This demonstrates your respect for and consideration of your partner's needs, wants, and feelings.

3. Reflect and evaluate if necessary

After discussing your concerns with each other and coming up with a solution together, reflect on what happened and evaluate whether or not the solution truly works for everyone involved. If it doesn't, talk about different solutions and reach another agreement so that everything is settled and everyone feels secure with how things turned out.

4: Make sure you both feel safe and secure

The final step to make sure that you both feel safe and secure is to make sure you have closure. Closure can be tough to achieve in relationships because it requires you to thank your partner for what they've done for you. It might also require a lot of crying, but your partner must know that they're loved and appreciated for who they are. They need to know that no matter how hard things get, you'll be there for them, and their feelings matter.

Show your partner you care about them by being open with them. Tell them that they're loved and appreciated, even if it's hard for you to admit it.

3. Take care of yourself

Taking care of yourself is also important in a relationship. Having a relationship with a fearful avoidant can be stressful for both parties. This is why it's crucial to look after your own needs. When you do so, you'll feel better, have more energy to invest in the relationship, and be able to concentrate on the positive aspects of being with a fearful avoidant rather than what they're doing incorrectly or forgetting to do.

How to do this:

a. Consider your needs

Focusing on your needs and feelings in a relationship with a fearful avoidant is important because their actions and behavior will affect your feelings, needs, and wants. If they ignore the needs that you have, this can lead to arguments and more issues that aren't resolved.

It's important to prioritize your needs and ensure they don't get ignored because this can lead to arguments and sometimes even abuse. This will make you feel insecure about the relationship, and it can also be stressful on your partner. When you prioritize your needs, it shows that you respect yourself. Additionally, it may help you relax and enjoy your time with your partner.

b. Vent your grief and frustration

Remember to vent your grief and frustration to ensure you don't bottle it all up inside.

Taking care of yourself means not bottling up feelings and emotions. Doing so will cause you to blow up on your partner in the long run, which isn't good for anyone involved. You'll have a lot of built-up frustrations, which will make you feel like yelling at them or exploding at the things they do that bother you the most. You won't be able to communicate how you feel to them because of this, and it will lead to fighting and arguments that aren't resolved. If you're fed up with your partner's behavior or habits, take a deep breath and tell them how you feel. Be calm, but be honest and straightforward; your feelings matter, and they need to know that you care enough to tell them how you feel.

c. Put yourself front and center

It's important to put yourself front and center when it comes to resolving conflicts. By doing this, you'll learn what it means to take care of yourself in a relationship, which will help you through the ups and downs of being with someone afraid of intimacy. Prioritizing your needs shows that you respect your partner for who they are.

Taking care of yourself is like a prize because it will give you more energy and confidence.

d. Keep your life interesting

Keep your life interesting and do things that bring you happiness, joy, and peace.

When you keep yourself busy or have a lot of hobbies, it shows your partner that your life doesn't revolve around them or their schedule. In addition, when you're happy and busy with your life, it shows that you respect yourself.

When you have a lot of hobbies, people will be able to see that you're happy and care about yourself. It shows that you aren't dependent on others for happiness, and will also encourage your partner to develop their own interests.

Taking care of yourself is important in every aspect of life. It's critical to realize that you cannot always make everyone happy and that you are not accountable for other someone else's emotions. Nobody can make your partner change their behavior and habits at will, but it is your right to decide what makes you happy and comfortable in a relationship.

If you maintain good communication with your partner and keep yourself healthy, effective communication with your partner will allow you to resolve disputes in a relationship quickly and enjoy the peaceful aspects of being with someone who is fearful avoidant.

CONCLUSION

A ttachment theory is a hermeneutic theory of human relationships based on the work of John Bowlby. Attachment theory holds that we form emotional connections with others in the first few years of our lives, and that those connections influence our emotional development as we grow up.

We all have an attachment style that matches how we relate to others. Attachment styles are formed in childhood through our early experiences with caregivers. A child with secure attachment grows up feeling safe and loved. This child can form relationships as an adult without fear of abandonment or rejection. A secure attachment is much more than just being able to depend on those that are around you. It is the ability to feel safe and comfortable around others; first to be able to depend on yourself and then to rely on others for support when needed. Having a secure attachment can help you in many ways as an adult, such as having a better understanding of love and how important it can be for your life. Many adults suffer from not having a secure attachment, a symptom of which is fearful avoidant attachment.

Fearful-avoidant attachment is a type of insecure attachment. Fearful-avoidant individuals are often caught up in thoughts of past events or what may happen to them in the future rather than being attuned to what is happening around them right now. They have difficulty seeing that most things they fear will never come true. They believe they have little control over most situations, making it difficult for them to trust anyone or anything in the world around them.

The relationship between a fearful-avoidant individual and a partner can be very difficult due to the way their attachment style leads them to perceive others. They often become overly negative about everything in their lives, including their partner. They are also very dependent on their partner. They are very easily upset when they do not get what they want from them, which makes it difficult for a fearful-avoidant individual to form healthy relationships. They are also very difficult to talk to and often do not believe what someone is telling them.

Fearful avoidants tend to push others away by being overly critical and avoiding their partner when they get into a relationship. This causes them to have a hard time being in healthy relationships because they are not able to open up to those who are closest to them. The fearful-avoidant attachment style tends to lead people to believe that they are in charge of their relationships, even when they are not. They will try to put a lot of pressure on themselves to make sure everything goes right in their relationship and may look at it as a burden because they feel like they have no way out. This can cause them to struggle with depression and emotional issues that can lead to physical pain. When fearful avoidants go through these negative emotions and actions, it can create a downward spiral.

The thoughts of the fearful-avoidant individual can greatly impact the way they see their relationships with others, as well as their relationship with themselves. They may develop poor physical and mental health, which may lead to them feeling insecure about everything. These individuals often feel like they cannot open up to others because of how uncomfortable it makes them feel, which causes more issues for them in every area of their life.

Fearful avoidants generally want to be in a relationship, but more than anything, they want to know that their partner will be loyal and kind. They will also feel scared at the same time.

Managing emotions is something fearful avoidants may struggle with. They must develop emotional restraint and learn to manage their fears and build self-confidence. Life is much easier when you have a strong sense of self-worth, which many people struggle with. Many things can be done to boost your self-esteem, and you must learn them to live a better life.

Your brain will be your best asset when it comes to getting through all of the different issues you have had in your life, and the more you use it, the better things will be for you. Additionally, knowing your attachment style is essential. Many do not understand their attachment style, which is why it will be hard for them to find love, but when you can see yourself for who you are, life will start to make more sense.

Although it won't necessarily be simple for you to find love, building a secure attachment will help you better understand your heart's desires and build a stronger sense of self-worth.

You can change and make your life better, but you have to be willing to look at the different options that are out there. If you want to find love in the future, learning about attachment is the first step to overcoming the challenges you face.